Awdeley's
Fraternitye of Vacabondes,
Harman's Caveat,
Haben's Sermon, &c.

Early English Text Society.
Extra Series. No. IX.

The Fraternitye of Vacabondes

BY JOHN AWDELEY

(LICENSED IN 1560-1, IMPRINTED THEN, AND IN 1565)

FROM THE EDITION OF 1575 IN THE BODLEIAN LIBRARY.

A Caueat or Warening for Commen Cursetors vulgarely called Vagabones

BY THOMAS HARMAN ESQUIERE,

FROM THE 3RD EDITION OF 1567, BELONGING TO HENRY HUTH, ESQ.

COLLATED WITH THE 2ND EDITION OF 1567 IN THE BODLEIAN LIBRARY, OXFORD, AND WITH THE REPRINT OF THE 4TH EDITION OF 1573.

A Sermon in Praise of Thiebes and Thievery

BY PARSON HABEN OR HYBERDYNE,

FROM THE LANSDOWNE MS. 98, AND COTTON VESP. A. 25.

THOSE PARTS OF

The Groundworke of Conny-catching (ed. 1592)

THAT DIFFER FROM *HARMAN'S CAUEAT.*

EDITED BY

EDWARD VILES & F. J. FURNIVALL.

LONDON:

PUBLISHED FOR THE EARLY ENGLISH TEXT SOCIETY
BY HUMPHREY MILFORD, OXFORD UNIVERSITY PRESS
AMEN HOUSE, E.C. 4

UNIVERSITY PRESS

Great Clarendon Street, Oxford OX2 6DP
United Kingdom

Oxford University Press is a department of the University of Oxford.
It furthers the University's objective of excellence in research, scholarship,
and education by publishing worldwide. Oxford is a registered trade mark of
Oxford University Press in the UK and in certain other countries

© The Early English Text Society 1869

The moral rights of the authors have been asserted

Database right Oxford University Press (maker)

First Edition published in 1869

All rights reserved. No part of this publication may be reproduced,
stored in a retrieval system, or transmitted, in any form or by any means,
without the prior permission in writing of Oxford University Press,
or as expressly permitted by law, or under terms agreed with the appropriate
reprographics rights organization. Enquiries concerning reproduction
outside the scope of the above should be sent to the Rights Department,
Oxford University Press, at the address above

You must not circulate this book in any other form
and you must impose this same condition on any acquirer

Published in the United States of America by Oxford University Press
198 Madison Avenue, New York, NY 10016, United States of America

British Library Cataloguing in Publication Data
Data available

Library of Congress Cataloging in Publication Data
Data available

Extra Series, 9

ISBN 978-0-85-991955-5

CONTENTS.

	PAGE
Preface	i
AWDELEY'S *Fraternitye*, not plagiarized from, but published 'a fewe yeares' before, Harman's *Caueat* ...	i
HARMAN'S *Caueat*: two states of the 2nd edition. The latter, now called the 3rd edition, is reprinted here ...	v
Piraters from Harman: Bynnyman, and G. Dewes	vi
Short account of Thomas Harman	vii
HARRISON'S quotation of Harman, and his account of English Vagabonds, and the punishments for them	xi
The Groundworke of Conny-catching is a reprint of Harman's *Caueat*, with an Introduction	xiv
DEKKER'S *Belman of London*: its borrowings from Harman	xiv
S. ROWLANDS'S *Martin Mark-all* shows up Dekker, and has new Cant words	xvi
DEKKER'S *Lanthorn and Candle-light* borrows from Harman: Canting Song from it	xix
The Caterpillers of this Nation anatomized	xxi
A Warning for Housebreakers	xxi
Street Robberies consider'd	xxii
Parson HABEN'S or HYBERDYNE'S *Sermon in Praise of Thieves and Thievery*	xxiv
Shares in the present work	xxiv
1. Awdeley's Fraternitye of Vacabondes, *with the* .xxv. Orders of Knaues (p. 12-16)	1-16
2. Harman's Caueat or Warreninge for Commen Cvrsetors bulgarely called Vagabones	17-91
3. Parson Haben's (or Hyberdyne's) Sermon in Praise of Thiebes and Thiebery	92-95
4. The Groundwork of Conny-catching: those parts that are not reprinted from Harman's *Caueat*	96-103
5. Index	104-111

PREFACE.

If the ways and slang of Vagabonds and Beggars interested Martin Luther enough to make him write a preface to the *Liber Vagatorum*[1] in 1528, two of the ungodly may be excused for caring, in 1869, for the old Rogues of their English land, and for putting together three of the earliest tracts about them. Moreover, these tracts are part of the illustrative matter that we want round our great book on Elizabethan England, Harrison's *Description of Britain,* and the chief of them is quoted by the excellent parson who wrote that book.

The first of these three tracts, Awdeley's *Fraternitye of Vacabondes,* has been treated by many hasty bibliographers, who can never have taken the trouble to read the first three leaves of Harman's book, as later than, and a mere pilfering from, Harman's *Caueat.* No such accusation, however, did Harman himself bring against the worthy printer-author (herein like printer-author Crowley, though he was preacher too,) who preceded him. In his Epistle dedicatory to the Countes of Shrewsbury, p. 20, below, Harman, after speaking of 'these wyly wanderers,' vagabonds, says in 1566 or 1567,

There was *a fewe yeares since* a small bréefe setforth of some zelous man to his countrey,—of whom I knowe not,—that made a lytle shewe of there names and vsage, and gaue a glymsinge lyghte, not sufficient to perswade of their peuishe peltinge and pickinge practyses, but well worthy of prayse.

[1] *Liber Vagatorum: Der Betler Orden:* First printed about 1514. Its first section gives a special account of the several orders of the 'Fraternity of Vagabonds;' the 2nd, sundry *notabilia* relating to them; the 3rd consists of a 'Rotwelsche Vocabulary,' or 'Canting Dictionary.' See a long notice in the Wiemarisches Jahrbuch, vol. 10; 1856. *Hotten's Slang Dictionary :* Bibliography.

This description of the 'small bréefe,' and the 'lytle shewe' of the 'names and vsage,' exactly suits Awdeley's tract; and the 'fewe yeares since' also suits the date of what may be safely assumed to be the first edition of the *Fraternitye*, by John Awdeley or John Sampson, or Sampson Awdeley,—for by all these names, says Mr Payne Collier, was our one man known:—

It may be disputed whether this printer's name were really Sampson, or Awdeley: he was made free of the Stationers' Company as Sampson, and so he is most frequently termed towards the commencement of the Register; but he certainly wrote and printed his name Awdeley or Awdelay; now and then it stands in the Register 'Sampson Awdeley.' It is the more important to settle the point, because . . . he was not only a printer, but a versifier,[1] and ought to have been included by Ritson in his *Bibliographica Poetica*. (Registers of the Stationers' Company, A.D. 1848, vol. i. p. 23.)

These verses of Awdeley's, or Sampson's, no doubt led to his 'small bréefe' being entered in the Stationers' Register as a 'ballett':

"1560-1. Rd. of John Sampson, for his lycense for pryntinge of a ballett called the description of vakaboundes .... iiij^d.

"[This entry seems to refer to an early edition of a very curious work, printed again by Sampson, alias Awdeley, in 1565, when it bore the following title, 'The fraternitie of vacabondes, as well of rufling vacabones as of beggerly,[2] as well of women as of men,[2] and as well of gyrles as of boyes, with their proper names and qualityes. Also the xxv. orders of knaves, otherwise called a quartten of knawes. Confirmed this yere by Cocke Lorel.' The edition without date mentioned by Dibdin (iv. 564) may have been that of the entry. Another impression by Awdeley, dated 1575 [which we reprint] is reviewed in the *British Bibliographer*, ii. 12, where it is asserted (as is very probable, though we are without distinct evidence of the fact) that the printer was the compiler of the book, and he certainly introduces it by three six-line stanzas. If this work came out originally in 1561, according to the entry, there is no doubt that it was the precursor of a very singular series of tracts on the same subject, which will be noticed in their proper places.]"—J. P. Collier, *Registers*, i. 42.

As above said, I take Harman's 'fewe yeares'—in 1566 or 7—to point to the 1561 edition of Awdeley, and not the 1565 ed. And as to Awdeley's authorship,—what can be more express than his own words,

---

[1] See the back of his title-page, p. 2, below.
[2] *as well* and *and as well* not in the title of the 1575 edition.

p. 2, below, that what the Vagabond caught at a Session confest as to 'both names and states of most and least of this their Vacabondes brotherhood,' *that*,—' at the request of a worshipful man, I ['The Printer,' that is, John Awdeley] have set it forth as well as I can.'

But if a doubt on Awdeley's priority to Harman exists in any reader's mind, let him consider this second reference by Harman to Awdeley (p. 60, below), not noticed by the bibliographers: "For-as-much as these two names, a Iarkeman and a Patrico, bée in *the old briefe of vacabonds*, and set forth as two kyndes of euil doers, you shall vnderstande that a Iarkeman hath his name of a *Iarke, which is a seale in their Language*, as one should *make writinges and set seales for lycences* and pasporte," and then turn to Awdeley's *Fraternitye of Vacabondes*, and there see, at page 5, below:

¶ A IACK MAN.

A Iackeman is he that can write and reade, and sometime speake latin. He vseth *to make counterfaite licences* which they call Gybes, *and sets to Seales, in their language called Iarkes*. (See also 'A Whipiacke,' p. 4.)

Let the reader then compare Harman's own description of a *Patrico*, p. 60, with that in 'the old *Briefe of Vacabonds*,' Awdeley, p. 6:

Awdeley.	Harman.
¶ A PATRIARKE CO.	there is a PATRICO ...
A Patriarke Co doth *make mariages*, & that is *vntill death depart* the maried folke.	whiche in their language is a priest, that should *make mariages tyll death dyd depart*.

And surely no doubt on the point will remain in his mind, though, if needed, a few more confirmations could be got, as

Awdeley (p. 4).	Harman (p. 44).
¶ A PALLIARD.	¶ A Pallyard.
A Palliard is he that goeth in a patched cloke, and hys Doxy goeth in like apparell.	These Palliardes .. go with patched clokes, and haue their Morts with them.

We may conclude, then, certainly, that Awdeley did not plagiarize Harman; and probably, that he first published his *Fraternitye* in 1561. The tract is a mere sketch, as compared with Harman's *Caueat*, though in its descriptions (p. 6—11) of 'A Curtesy Man,'

'A Cheatour or Fingerer,' and 'A Ring-Faller' (one of whom tried his tricks on me in Gower-street about ten days ago), it gives as full a picture as Harman does of the general run of his characters. The edition of 1575 being the only one accessible to us, our trusty Oxford copier, Mr George Parker, has read the proofs with the copy in the Bodleian.

Let no one bring a charge of plagiarizing Awdeley, against Harman, for the latter, as has been shown, referred fairly to Awdeley's '*small breefe*' or '*old briefe of vacabonds,*' and wrote his own "bolde Beggars booke" (p. 91) from his own long experience with them.

Harman's *Caueat* is too well-known and widely valued a book to need description or eulogy here. It is *the* standard work on its subject,—'these rowsey, ragged, rabblement of rakehelles' (p. 19)— and has been largely plundered by divers literary cadgers. No copy of the first edition seems to be known to bibliographers. It was published in 1566 or 1567,—probably the latter year,[1]—and must (I conclude) have contained less than the second, as in that's 'Harman to the Reader,' p. 28, below, he says 'well good reader, I meane not to be tedyous vnto the, but haue added fyue or sixe more tales, because some of them weare doune whyle my booke was fyrste in the presse.' He speaks again of his first edition at p. 44, below, 'I had the best geldinge stolen oute of my pasture, that I had amongst others, whyle this boke was *first a printynge;*' and also at p. 51, below, 'Apon Alhol enday in the morning last anno domini 1566, or my booke was halfe printed, I meane *the first impression.*' All Hallows' or All Saints' Day is November 1.

The edition called the second[2], also bearing date in 1567, is known to us in two states, the latter of which I have called the third edition. The first state of the second edition is shown by the Bodleian copy, which is 'Augmented and inlarged by the fyrst author here of,' and has, besides smaller differences specified in the footnotes in our pages, this great difference, that the arrangement of 'The Names of

[1] Compare the anecdote, p. 66, 68, 'the *last* sommer, Anno Domini, 1566.'
[2] 'now at this seconde Impression,' p. 27; 'Whyle this second Impression was in printinge,' p. 87.

the Vpright Men, Roges, and Pallyards' is not alphabetical, by the first letter of the Christian names, as in the second state of the second edition (which I call the third edition), but higgledy-piggledy, or, at least, without attention to the succession of initials either of Christian or Sur-names, thus, though in three columns:

¶ VPRIGHT MEN.

Richard Brymmysh. Robert Gerse.
John Myllar. Gryffen.
Wel arayd Richard. Richard Barton.
John Walchman. John Braye.
Wylliam Chamborne. Thomas Cutter.
Bryan Medcalfe. Dowzabell skylfull in fence.
[&c.]

¶ ROGES.

Harry Walles with the little mouth. Lytle Robyn.
John Waren. Lytle Dycke.
Richard Brewton. Richard Iones.
Thomas Paske. Lambart Rose.
George Belbarby. Harry Mason.
Humfrey Warde. Thomas Smithe with the skal skyn.
[&c.]

¶ PALLYARDS.

Nycholas Newton carieth a fayned lycence. Edward Heyward, hath his Morte following hym Whiche fayneth ye crank.
Bashforde.
Robart Lackley. Preston.
Wylliam Thomas. Robart Canloke.
[&c.]

This alone settles the priority of the Bodley edition, as no printer, having an index alphabetical, would go and muddle it all again, even for a lark. Moreover, the other collations confirm this priority. The colophon of the Bodley edition is dated A. D. 1567, 'the eight of January;' and therefore A. D. 1567-8.

The second state of the second edition—which state I call the third edition—is shown by the copy which Mr Henry Huth has, with his never-failing generosity, lent us to copy and print from. It omits 'the eight of January,' from the colophon, and has 'Anno Domini 1567' only. Like the 2nd edition (or 2 A), this 3rd edition (or 2 B) has the statement on p. 87, below: 'Whyle this second Impression was in printinge, it fortuned that Nycholas Blunte, who called hym selfe Nycholan Gennyns, a counterefet Cranke, that is spoken of in this booke, was fonde begging in the whyte fryers on Newe yeares day last past, Anno domini .1567, and commytted vnto a offescer, who caried hym vnto the depetye of the ward, which commytted hym vnto the counter;' and this brings both the 2nd and 3rd editions (or 2 A and 2 B) to the year 1568, modern style. The 4th edition, so far as I know, was published in 1573, and was reprinted by Machell Stace (says Bohn's Lowndes) in 1814. From that reprint Mr W. M. Wood has made a collation of words, not letters, for us with the 3rd edition. The chief difference of the 4th edition is its extension of the story of the 'dyssembling Cranke,' Nycholas Genings, and 'the Printar of this booke' Wylliam Gryffith (p. 53-6, below), which extension is given in the footnotes to pages 56 and 57 of our edition. We were obliged to reprint this from Stace's reprint of 1814, as our searchers could not find a copy of the 4th edition of 1573 in either the British Museum, the Bodleian, or the Cambridge University Library.

Thus much about our present edition. I now hark back to the first, and the piracies of it or the later editions, mentioned in Mr J. P. Collier's *Registers of the Stationers' Company*, i. 155-6, 166.

"1566-7 Rd. of William Greffeth, for his lycense for printinge of a boke intituled a Caviat for commen Corsetors, vulgarly called Vagabons, by Thomas Harman . . . . iiij^d.

"[No edition of Harman's 'Caveat or Warning for common Cursetors,' of the date of 1566, is known, although it is erroneously mentioned in the introductory matter to the reprint in 1814, from H. Middleton's impression of 1573. It was the forerunner of various later works of the same kind, some of which were plundered from it without acknowledgment, and attributed to the celebrated Robert Greene. Copies of two editions in 1567, by Griffith, are extant, and, in all probability, it was the first time it appeared in print: Griffith entered it at Stationers' Hall, as above, in 1566, in order that he might publish it in 1567. Harman's work was preceded by several ballads relating to vagabonds, the earliest of which is entered on p. 42 [Awdeley, p. ii. above]. On a subsequent page (166) is inserted a curious entry regarding 'the boke of Rogges,' or Rogues.]

"1566-7. For Takynge of Fynes as foloweth. Rd. of Henry

Bynnyman, for his fyne for undermy[n]dinge and procurynge, as moche as in hym ded lye, a Copye from wylliam greffeth, called the boke of Rogges . . . . iij^s.

"[This was certainly Harman's 'Caveat or Warning for Common Cursetors'; and here we see Bynneman fined for endeavouring to *undermine* Griffith by procuring the copy of the work, in order that Bynneman might print and publish it instead of Griffith, his rival in business. The next item may show that Gerard Dewes had also printed the book, no doubt without license, but the memorandum was crossed out in the register.]

"Also, there doth remayne in the handes of Mr Tottle and Mr Gonneld, then wardens, the somme of iij^{li}. vij^s. viij^d., wherto was Recevyd of garrad dewes for pryntinge of the boke of Rogges in a° 1567 . . . . ij^{li}. vj^s. viij^d.

"[All tends to prove the desire of stationers to obtain some share of the profits of a work, which, as we have already shown, was so well received, that Griffith published two editions of it in 1567.]"

The fact is, the book was so interesting that it made its readers thieves, as 'Jack Sheppard' has done in later days. The very woodcutter cheated Harman of the hind legs of the horse on his title, prigged two of his prauncer's props (p. 42).

To know the keen inquiring Social Reformer, Thomas Harman, the reader must go to his book. He lived in the country (p. 34, foot), in [Crayford] Kent (p. 30, p. 35), near a heath (p. 35), near Lady Elizabeth Shrewsbury's parish (p. 19), not far from London (p. 30, p. 35) ; ' he lodged at the White Friars within the cloister ' (p. 51), seemingly while he was having his book printed (p. 53), and had his servant there with him (*ib.*) ; ' he knew London well ' (p. 54, &c.) ; and in Kent ' beinge placed as a poore gentleman,' he had in 1567, ' kepte a house these twenty yeares, where vnto pouerty dayely hath and doth repayre,' and where, being kept at home ' through sickenes, he talked dayly with many of these wyly wanderars, as well men and wemmen, as boyes and gyrles,' whose tricks he has so pleasantly set down for us. He did not, though, confine his intercourse with vagabonds to talking, for he says of some, p. 48,

¶ Some tyme they counterfet the seale of the Admiraltie. I haue diuers tymes taken a waye from them their lycences of both sortes, wyth suche money as they haue gathered, and haue confiscated the same to the pouerty nigh adioyninge to me. p. 51-6.

Our author also practically exposed these tricks, as witness his hunting out the Cranke, Nycholas Genings, and his securing the vagabond's 13s. and 4d. for the poor of Newington parish, p. 51-6, his making the deaf and dumb beggar hear and speak, p. 58-9 (and securing his money too for the poor). But he fed deserving beggars, see p. 66, p. 20.

Though Harman tells us 'Eloquence haue I none, I neuer was acquaynted with the Muses, I neuer tasted of Helycon' (p. 27-8), yet he could write verses—though awfully bad ones: see them at pages 50 and 89-91, below, perhaps too at p. 26 [1];—he knew Latin—see his comment on Cursetors and Vagabone, p. 27; his *una voce*, p 43; perhaps his 'Argus eyes,' p. 54; his *omnia venalia Rome*, p 60; his *homo*, p. 73; he quotes St Augustine (and the Bible), p. 24; &c.;—he studied the old Statutes of the Realm (p. 27); he liked proverbs (see the Index); he was once 'in commission of the peace,' as he says, and judged malefactors, p. 60, though he evidently was not a Justice when he wrote his book; he was a 'gentleman,' says Harrison (see p. xii. below); 'a Iustice of Peace in Kent,[2] in Queene Marie's daies,' says Samuel Rowlands;[3] he bore arms (of heraldry), and had them duly stamped on his pewter dishes (p. 35); he had at least one old 'tennant who customably a greate tyme went twise in the weeke to London, (over Blacke Heathe) eyther wyth fruite or with pescoddes' (p. 30); he hospitably asked his visitors to dinner (p. 45); he had horses in his pasture,[4] the best gelding of which the Pryggers of Prauncers prigged (p. 44); he had an unchaste cow that went to bull every month (p. 67, if his ownership is not chaff here); he had in his 'well-house on the backe side of

[1] Mr J. P. Collier (*Bibliographical Catalogue*, i. 365) has little doubt that the verses at the back of the title-page of Harman's *Caveat* were part of "a ballad intituled a description of the nature of a birchen broom" entered at Stationers' Hall to William Griffith, the first printer of the *Caveat*.
[2] Cp. Kente, p. 37, 43, 48, 61, 63, 66, 68, 77, &c. Moreover, the way in which he, like a Norfolk or Suffolk man, speaks of *shires*, points to a liver in a non -*shire*.
[3] In *Martin Mark-all, Beadle of Bridewell*, 1610, quoted below, at p. xvii.
[4] Compare his 'ride to Dartforde to speake with a priest there,' p. 57.

his house, a great cawdron of copper' which the beggars stole (p. 34-5); he couldn't keep his linen on his hedges or in his rooms, or his pigs and poultry from the thieves (p. 21); he hated the 'rascal rabblement' of them (p. 21), and 'the wicked parsons that keepe typlinge Houses in all shires, where they haue succour and reliefe'; and, like a wise and practical man, he set himself to find out and expose all their 'vndecent, dolefull [guileful] dealing, and execrable exercyses' (p. 21) to the end that they might be stopt, and sin and wickedness might not so much abound, and thus 'this Famous Empyre be in more welth, and better florysh, to the inestymable joye and comfort' of his great Queen, Elizabeth, and the 'vnspeakable .. reliefe and quietnes of minde, of all her fayth-full Commons and Subiectes.' The right end, and the right way to it. We've some like you still, Thomas Harman, in our Victorian time. May their number grow!

Thus much about Harman we learn from his book and his literary contemporaries and successors. If we now turn to the historian of his county, Hasted, we find further interesting details about our author: 1, that he lived in Crayford parish, next to Erith, the Countess of Shrewsbury's parish; 2, that he inherited the estates of Ellam, and Maystreet, and the manor of Mayton or Maxton; 3, that he was the grandson of Henry Harman, Clerk of the Crown, who had for his arms 'Argent, a chevron between 3 scalps sable,' which were no doubt those stampt on our Thomas's pewter dishes; 4, that he had a 'descendant,'—a son, I presume—who inherited his lands, and three daughters, one of whom, Bridget, married Henry Binneman—? not the printer, about 1565-85 A.D., p. vi-vii, above.

Hasted in his description of the parish of Crayford, speaking of Ellam, a place in the parish, says:—

"In the 16th year of K. Henry VII. John Ellam alienated it (the seat of Ellam) to Henry Harman, who was then Clerk of the Crown,[1] and

[1] "John Harman, Esquyer, one of the gentilmen hushers of the Chambre of our soverayn Lady the Quene, and the excellent Lady Dame Dorothye Gwydott, widow, late of the town of Southampton, married Dec. 21, 1557." (Extract from the register of the parish of Stratford Bow, given in p. 499, vol. iii. of Lysons's *Environs of London.*

THOMAS HARMAN'S FAMILY AND ESTATES.

who likewise purchased an estate called Maystreet here, of Cowley and Bulbeck, of Bulbeck-street in this parish, in the 20th year of King Edward IV.[1] On his decease, William Harman, his son, possessed both these estates.[2] On his decease they descended to Thomas Harman, esq., his son; who, among others, procured his lands to be disgavelled, by the act of the 2 & 3 Edw. VI.[3] He married Millicent, one of the daughters of Nicholas Leigh, of Addington, in the county of Surry, esq.[4] His descendant, William Harman, sold both these places in the reign of K. James I. to Robert Draper, esqr."—*History of Kent*, vol. i. p. 209.

The manor of Maxton, in the parish of Hougham " passed to Hobday, and thence to Harman, of Crayford; from which name it was sold by Thomas Harman to Sir James Hales. . . . . William Harman held the manor of Mayton, alias Maxton, with its appurtenances, of the Lord Cheney, as of his manor of Chilham, by Knight's service. Thomas Harman was his son and heir: Rot. Esch. 2 Edw. VI."—Hasted's *History of Kent*, vi. p. 47.

"It is laid down as a rule, that nothing but an act of parliament can change the nature of gavelkind lands; and this has occasioned several [acts], for the purpose of disgavelling the possessions of divers gentlemen in this county. . . . . One out of several statutes made for this purpose is the 3rd of Edw. VI."—Hasted's *History of Kent*, vol. i. p. cxliii.

And in the list of names given,—taken from Robinson's *Gavelkind*—twelfth from the bottom stands that of THOMAS HARMAN.

Of Thomas Harman's aunt, Mary, Mrs William Lovelace, we find: "John Lovelace, esq., and William Lovelace, his brother, possessed this manor and seat (Bayford-Castle) between them; the latter of whom resided at Bayford, where he died in the 2nd year of K. Edward VI., leaving issue by Mary his wife, daughter of William Harman, of Crayford, seven sons. . . . "—Hasted's *History of Kent*, vol. ii. p. 612.

The rectory of the parish of Deal was bestowed by the Archbishop on Roger Harman in 1544 (*Hasted*, vol. iv. p. 171).

Harman-street is the name of a farm in the parish of Ash (*Hasted*, vol. iii. p. 691).

[1] Philipott, p. 108. Henry Harman bore for his arms—Argent, a chevron between 3 scalps sable.
[2] Of whose daughters, Mary married John, eldest son of Wm. Lovelace, of Hever in Kingsdown, in this county; and Elizabeth married John Lennard, Prothonotary, and afterwards *Custos Brevium* of the Common Pleas. See Chevening.
[3] See Robinson's Gavelkind, p. 300.
[4] She was of consanguinity to Abp. Chicheley. *Stemm. Chich.* No. 106. Thomas Harman had three daughters: Anne, who married Wm. Draper, of Erith, and lies buried there; Mary, who married Thomas Harrys; and Bridget, who was the wife of Henry Binneman. *Ibid.*

The excellent parson, William Harrison, in his 'Description of England,' prefixed to Holinshed's Chronicles (edit. 1586), quotes Harman fairly enough in his chapter "Of prouision made for the poore," Book II, chap. 10.[1] And as he gives a statement of the sharp punishment enacted for idle rogues and vagabonds by the Statutes of Elizabeth, I take a long extract from his said chapter. After speaking of those who are made 'beggers through other mens occasion,' and denouncing the grasping landlords 'who make them so, and wipe manie out of their occupiengs,' Harrison goes on to those who are beggars 'through their owne default' (p. 183, last line of col. 1, ed. 1586):

"Such as are idle beggers through their owne default are of two sorts, and continue their estates either by casuall or meere voluntarie meanes: those that are such by casuall means [2] are in the beginning [2] iustlie to be referred either to the first or second sort of poore [2] afore mentioned [2]; but, degenerating into the thriftlesse sort, they doo what they can to continue their miserie; and, with such impediments as they haue, to straie and wander about, as creatures abhorring all labour and euerie honest excercise. Certes, I call these casuall meanes, not in respect of the originall of their pouertie, but of the continuance of the same, from whence they will not be deliuered, such[3] is their owne vngratious lewdnesse and froward disposition. The voluntarie meanes proceed from outward causes, as by making of corosiues, and applieng the same to the more fleshie parts of their bodies; and also laieng of ratsbane, sperewort, crowfoot, and such like vnto their whole members, thereby to raise pitifull[4] and odious sores, and mooue [2] the harts of [2] the goers by such places where they lie, to [5] yerne at [5] their miserie, and therevpon [2] bestow large almesse vpon them.[6] How artificiallie they beg, what forcible speech, and how they select and choose out words of vehemencie, whereby they doo in maner coniure or adiure the goer by to pitie their cases, I passe ouer to remember, as iudging the name of God and Christ to be more conuersant in the mouths of none, and yet the presence of the heuenlie maiestie further off from no men than from this vngratious companie. Which maketh me to thinke, that punishment is farre meeter for them than liberalitie or almesse, and sith Christ willeth vs cheeflie to haue a regard to himselfe and his poore members.

"Vnto this nest is another sort to be referred, more sturdie than the rest, which, hauing sound and perfect lims, doo yet, notwithstanding

---

[1] In the first edition of Holinshed (1577) this chapter is the 5th in Book III. of Harrison's *Description*.

[2-2] Not in ed. 1577.   [3] *thorow* in ed. 1577.

[4] *piteous* in ed. 1577.   [5-5] *lament* in ed. 1577.

[6] The remainder of this paragraph is not in ed. 1577.

sometime counterfeit the possession of all sorts of diseases. Diuerse times in their apparell also [1] they will be like seruing men or laborers: oftentimes they can plaie the mariners, and seeke for ships which they neuer lost.[2] But, in fine, they are all theeues and caterpillers in the commonwealth, and, by the word of God not permitted to eat, sith they doo but licke the sweat from the true laborers' browes, *and* beereue the godlie poore of that which is due vnto them, to mainteine their excesse, consuming the charitie of well-disposed people bestowed vpon them, after a most wicked [3] *and* detestable maner.

"It is not yet full threescore [4] yeares since this trade began: but how it hath prospered since that time, it is easie to iudge; for they are now supposed, of one sex and another, to amount vnto aboue 10,000 persons, as I haue heard reported. Moreouer, in counterfeiting the Egyptian roges, they haue deuised a language among themselues, which they name *Canting* (but other pedlers French)—a speach compact thirtie yeares since of English, and a great number of od words of their owne deuising, without all order or reason: and yet such is it as none but themselues are able to vnderstand. The first deuiser thereof was hanged by the necke,—a iust reward, no doubt, for his deserts, and a common end to all of that profession. A gentleman, also, of late hath taken great paines to search out the secret practises of this vngratious rabble. And among other things he setteth downe and describeth [5] three *and* twentie [5] sorts of them, whose names it shall not be amisse to remember, wherby ech one may [6] take occasion to read and know as also by his industrie [6] what wicked people they are, and what villanie remaineth in them.

[Thomas Harman.]

"The seuerall disorders and degrees amongst our idle vagabonds:—

1. Rufflers.
2. Vprightmen.
3. Hookers or Anglers.
4. Roges.
5. Wild Roges.
6. Priggers of Prancers.
7. Palliards.
8. Fraters.
9. Abrams.
10. Freshwater mariners, or Whip-[iacks.
11. Dummerers.
12. Drunken tinkers.
13. Swadders, or Pedlers.
14. Iarkemen, or Patricoes.

Of Women kinde—

1. Demanders for glimmar, or fire.
2. Baudie Baskets.
3. Mortes.
4. Autem mortes.
5. Walking mortes.
6. Doxes.
7. Delles.
8. Kinching Mortes.
9. Kinching cooes.[7]

[1] Not in ed. 1577.   [2] Compare *Harman*, p. 48.
[3] The 1577 ed. inserts *horrible*.
[4] The 1577 ed. reads *fifty*.
[5-5] The 1577 ed. reads 22, which is evidently an error.
[6-6] For these words the 1577 ed. reads *gather*.
[7] The above list is taken from the titles of the chapters in Harman's *Caueat*.

"The punishment that is ordeined for this kind of people is verie sharpe, and yet it can not restreine them from their gadding: wherefore the end must needs be martiall law, to be exercised vpon them as vpon theeues, robbers, despisers of all lawes, and enimies to the common-wealth *and* welfare of the land. What notable roberies, pilferies, murders, rapes, and stealings of yoong[1] children, [2]burning, breaking and disfiguring their lims to make them pitifull in the sight of the people,[2] I need not to rehearse; but for their idle roging about the countrie, the law ordeineth this maner of correction. The roge being apprehended, committed to prison, and tried in the next assises (whether they be of gaole deliuerie or sessions of the peace) if he happen to be conuicted for a vagabond either by inquest of office, or the testimonie of two honest and credible witnesses vpon their oths, he is then immediatlie adiudged to be greeuouslie whipped and burned through the gristle of the right eare, with an hot iron of the compasse of an inch about, as a manifesta-tion of his wicked life, and due punishment receiued for the same. And this iudgement is to be executed vpon him, except some honest person woorth fiue pounds in the queene's books in goods, or twentie shillings in lands, or some rich housholder to be allowed by the iustices, will be bound in recognisance to reteine him in his seruice for one whole yeare. If he be taken the second time, and proued to haue forsaken his said seruice, he shall then be whipped againe, bored likewise through the other eare and set to seruice: from whence if he depart before a yeare be expired, and happen afterward to be attached againe, he is con-demned to suffer paines of death as a fellon (except before excepted) without benefit of clergie or sanctuarie, as by the statute dooth appeare. Among roges and idle persons finallie, we find to be comprised all proctors that go vp and downe with counterfeit licences, coosiners, and such as gad about the countrie, vsing vnlawfull games, practisers of physiognomie, and palmestrie, tellers of fortunes, fensers, plaiers,[3] minstrels, iugglers, pedlers, tinkers, pretensed[4] schollers, shipmen, prisoners gathering for fees, and others, so oft as they be taken without sufficient licence. From [5]among which companie our bearewards are not excepted, and iust cause: for I haue read that they haue either voluntarilie, or for want of power to master their sauage beasts, beene occasion of the death and deuoration of manie children in sundrie coun-tries by which they haue passed, whose parents neuer knew what was become of them. And for that cause there is *and* haue beene manie sharpe lawes made for bearwards in Germanie, wherof you may read in other. But to our roges.[5] Each one also that harboreth or aideth them with meat or monie, is taxed and compelled to fine with the queene's maiestie for euerie time that he dooth so succour them, as it

---

[1] Not in the 1577 ed.

[2-2] These words are substituted for *which they disfigure to begg withal* in the 1577 ed.

[3] The 1577 ed. inserts *bearwards*.   [4] Not in 1577 ed.

[5-5] These three sentences are not in 1577 ed.

shall please the iustices of peace to assigne, so that the taxation exceed not twentie shillings, as I haue beene informed. And thus much of the poore, *and* such prouision as is appointed for them within the realme of England."

Among the users of Harman's book, the chief and coolest was the author of *The groundworke of Conny-catching*, 1592, who **wrote a few introductory pages, and then quietly reprinted almost all Harman's book** with an 'I leaue you now vnto those which by Maister Harman are discouered' (p. 103, below). By this time Harman was no doubt dead.—Who will search for his Will in the Wills Office? —Though Samuel Rowlands was alive, he did not show up this early appropriator of Harman's work as he did a later one. As a kind of Supplement to the *Caueat*, I have added, as the 4th tract in the present volume, such parts of the *Groundworke of Conny-catching* as are not reprinted from Harman. The *Groundworke* has been attributed to Robert Greene, but on no evidence (I believe) except Greene's having written a book in three Parts on Conny-catching, 1591-2, and 'A Disputation betweene a Hee Conny-catcher and a Shee Conny-catcher, whether a Theafe or a Whore is most hvrtfull in Cousonage to the Common-wealth,' 1592.[1] Hearne's copy of the *Groundworke* is bound up in the 2nd vol. of Greene's Works, among George III.'s books in the British Museum, as if it really was Greene's.

Another pilferer from Harman was Thomas Dekker, in his *Belman of London*, 1608, of which three editions were published in the same year (*Hazlitt*). But Samuel Rowlands found him out and showed him up. From the fifth edition of the Belman, the earliest that our copier, Mr W. M. Wood, could find in the British Museum, he has drawn up the following account of the book :

> *The Belman of London. Bringing to Light the most notorious Villanies that are now practised in the Kingdome. Profitable for Gentlemen, Lawyers, Merchants, Citizens, Farmers, Masters of Housholds, and all sorts of Servants to mark, and delightfull for all Men to Reade.*
> Lege, Perlege, Relege.
> *The fift Impression, with new additions. Printed at London by Miles Flesher.* 1640

[1] Hazlitt's *Hand Book*, p. 241.

On the back of the title-page, after the table of contents, the eleven following 'secret villanies' are described, severally, as

"Cheating Law	Bernard's Lawe.
Vincent's Law.	The black Art.
Curbing Law.	Prigging Law.
Lifting Law.	High Law.
Sacking Law.	Frigging Law.

Fiue Iumpes at Leape-frog."

After a short description of the four ages of the world, there is an account of a feast, at which were present all kinds of vagabonds. Dekker was conveyed, by 'an old nimble-tong'd beldam, who seemed to haue the command of the place,' to an upper loft, 'where, vnseene, I might, through a wooden Latice that had prospect of the dining roome, both see and heare all that was to be done or spoken.'

'The whole assembly being thus gathered together, one, amongest the rest, who tooke vpon him a Seniority ouer the rest, charged euery man to answer to his name, to see if the Iury were full:—the Bill by which hee meant to call them beeing a double Iug of ale (that had the spirit of *Aquavitæ* in it, it smelt so strong), and that hee held in his hand. Another, standing by, with a toast, nutmeg, and ginger, ready to cry *Vous avez* as they were cald, and all that were in the roome hauing single pots by the eares, which, like Pistols, were charged to goe off so soone as euer they heard their names. This Ceremony beeing set abroach, an Oyes was made. But he that was Rector Chory (the Captain of the Tatterdemalions) spying one to march vnder his Colours, that had neuer before serued in those lowsie warres, paused awhile (after hee had taken his first draught, to tast the dexterity of the liquor), and then began, Iustice-like, to examine this yonger brother vpon interrogatories.'

This yonger brother is afterwards 'stalled to the rogue;' and the 'Rector Chory[1]' instructs him in his duties, and tells him the names and degrees of the fraternity of vagabonds. Then comes the feast, after which, 'one who tooke vpon him to be speaker to the whole house,' began, as was the custom of their meeting, 'to make an oration in praise of Beggery, and of those that professe the trade,' which done, all the company departed, leaving the 'old beldam' and Dekker the only occupants of the room.

'The spirit of her owne mault walkt in her brain-pan, so that, what with the sweetnes of gaines which shee had gotten by her Marchant

---

[1] Leader of the Choir, Captain of the Company.

Venturers, and what with the fumes of drinke, which set her tongue in going, I found her apt for talke; and, taking hold of this opportunity, after some intreaty to discouer to mee what these vpright men, rufflers and the rest were, with their seuerall qualities and manners of life, Thus shee began.'

And what she tells Dekker is taken, all of it, from Harman's book.

Afterwards come accounts of the five 'Laws' and five jumps at leap-frog mentioned on the back of the title-page, and which is quoted above, p. xv.

Lastly 'A short Discourse of Canting,' which is, entirely, taken from Harman, pages 84—87, below.

As I have said before, Dekker was shown up for his pilferings from Harman by Samuel Rowlands, who must, says Mr Collier in his Bibliographical Catalogue, have published his *Martin Mark-all, Beadle of Bridewell*, in or before 1609,—though no edition is known to us before 1610,—because Dekker in an address 'To my owne Nation' in his *Lanthorne and Candle-light*, which was published in 1609, refers to Rowlands as a 'Beadle of Bridewell.' 'You shall know him,' (says Dekker, speaking of a rival author, [that is, Samuel Rowlands] whom he calls 'a Usurper') 'by his Habiliments, for (by the furniture he weares) hee will bee taken for *a Beadle of Bridewell*.' That this 'Usurper' was Rowlands, we know by the latter's saying in *Martin Mark-all*, leaf E, i back, 'although he (the Bel-man, that is, Dekker) is bold to call me an *vsurper;* for so he doth in his last round.'

Well, from this treatise of Rowlands', Mr Wood has made the following extracts relating to Dekker and Harman, together with Rowlands's own list of slang words not in Dekker or Harman, and 'the errour in his [Dekker's] words, and true englishing of the same:'

Martin Mark-all, Beadle of Bridewell; his defence and Answere to the Belman of London, Discouering the long-concealed Originall and Regiment of Rogues, when they first began to take head, and how they haue succeeded one the other successiuely vnto the sixe and twentieth yeare of King Henry the eight, gathered out of the Chronicle of Crackeropes, and (as they terme it) the Legend of Lossels. By S[amuel] R[owlands].

Orderunt peccare boni virtutis amore,
Orderunt peccare mali formidine pœnæ.

London
Printed for Iohn Budge and Richard Bonian. 1610.

'Martin Mark-all, his Apologie to the Bel-man of London. There hath been of late dayes great paines taken on the part of the good old Bel-man of London, in discouering, as hee thinks, a new-found Nation and People. Let it be so for this time : hereupon much adoe was made in setting forth their liues, order of liuing, method of speech, and vsuall meetings, with diuers other things thereunto appertaining. These volumes and papers, now spread euerie where, so that euerie Iacke-boy now can say as well as the proudest of that fraternitie, "will you wapp for a wyn, or tranie for a make?" The gentle Company of Cursitours began now to stirre, and looke about them ; and hauing gathered together a Conuocation of Canting Caterpillars, as wel in the North parts at the Diuels arse apeake,[1] as in the South, they diligently enquired, and straight search was made, whether any had reuolted from that faithles fellowship. Herupon euery one gaue his verdict: some supposed that it might be some one that, hauing ventured to farre beyond wit and good taking heede, was fallen into the hands of the Magistrate, and carried to the trayning Cheates, where, in shew of a penitent heart, and remoarse of his good time ill spent, turned the cocke, and let out all : others thought it might be some spie-knaue that, hauing little to doe, tooke vpon him the habite and forme of an Hermite ; and so, by dayly commercing and discoursing, learned in time the mysterie and knowlege of this ignoble profession : and others, because it smelt of a study, deemed it to be some of their owne companie, that had been at some free-schoole, and belike, because hee would be handsome against a good time, tooke pen and inke, and wrote of that subiect ; thus, *Tot homines, tot sententiæ,* so many men, so many mindes. And all because the spightfull Poet would not set too his name. At last vp starts an old Cacodemicall Academicke with his frize bonnet, and giues them al to know, that this invectiue was set foorth, made, and printed Fortie yeeres agoe. And being then called, 'A caueat for Cursitors,' is now newly printed, and termed, 'The Bel-man of London,' made at first by one Master Harman, a Iustice of Peace in Kent, in Queene Marie's daies,—he being then about ten yeeres of age.' Sign. A. 2.

'They (the vagabonds) haue a language among themselues, composed of *omnium gatherum ;* a glimering whereof, one of late daies hath endeuoured to manifest, as farre as his Authour is pleased to be an in-

---

[1] Where at this day the Rogues of the North part, once euerie three yeeres, assemble in the night, because they will not be seene and espied ; being a place, to those that know it, verie fit for that purpos,—it being hollow, and made spacious vnder ground ; at first, by estimation, halfe a mile in compasse ; but it hath such turnings and roundings in it, that a man may easily be lost if hee enter not with a guide.

telligencer. The substance whereof he leaueth for those that will dilate thereof; enough for him to haue the praise, other the paines, notwithstanding *Harman's* ghost continually clogging his conscience with *Sic Vos non Vobis.*'—Sign. C. 3 back.[1]

'Because the Bel-man entreateth any that is more rich in canting, to lend him better or more with variety, he will repay his loue double, I haue thought good, not only to shew his errour in some places in setting downe olde wordes vsed fortie yeeres agoe, before he was borne, for wordes that are vsed in these dayes (although he is bold to call me an vsurper (for so he doth in his last round), and not able to maintayne the title, but haue enlarged his Dictionary (or *Master Harman's*) with such wordes as I thinke hee neuer heard of (and yet in vse too); but not out of vaine glorie, as his ambition is, but, indeede, as an experienced souldier that hath deerely paid for it: and therefore it shall be honour good enough for him (if not too good) to come vp with the Reare (I doe but shoote your owne arrow back againe), and not to haue the leading of the Van as he meanes to doe, although small credite in the end will redound to eyther. You shall know the wordes not set in eyther his Dictionaries by this marke §: and for shewing the errour in his words, and true englishing of the same and other, this marke ¶ shall serue

§ Abram, madde
§ He maunds Abram, he begs as a madde man
¶ Bung, is now vsed for a pocket, heretofore for a purse
§ Budge a beake, runne away
§ A Bite, secreta mulierum
§ Crackmans, the hedge
§ To Castell, to see or looke
§ A Roome Cuttle, a sword
§ A Cuttle bung, a knife to cut a purse
§ Chepemans, Cheape-side market
¶ Chates, the Gallowes: here he mistakes both the simple word, because he so found it printed, not knowing the true originall thereof, and also in the compound; as for *Chates*, it should be *Cheates*, which word is vsed generally for things, as *Tip me that Cheate*, Giue me that thing: so that if you will make a word for the Gallous, you must put thereto this word *treyning*, which signifies

[1] Of the above passages, Dekker speaks in the following manner:—"There is an Vsurper, that of late hath taken vpon him the name of the Belman; but being not able to maintaine that title, hee doth now call himselfe the Bel-mans brother; his ambition is (rather out of vaine-glory then the true courage of an experienced Souldier) to haue the leading of the Van; but it shall be honor good enough for him (if not too good) to come vp with the Rere. You shall know him by his Habiliments, for (by the furniture he weares) he will be taken for a *Beadle of Bridewell*. It is thought he is rather a Newter then a friend to the cause: and therefore the Bel-man doth here openly protest that hee comes into the field as no fellow in armes with him."—*O per se O* (1612 edit.), sign. A. 2.

hanging; and so *treyning cheate* is as much to say, hanging things, or the Gallous, and not *Chates*.

§ A fflicke, a Theefe
§ Famblers, a paire of Gloues
§ Greenemans, the fields
§ Gilkes for the gigger, false keyes for the doore or picklockes
§ Gracemans, Gratious streete market
§ Iockam, a man's yard
§ Ian, a purse
§ Iere, a turd
§ Lugges, eares
§ Loges, a passe or warrant
§ A Feager of Loges, one that beggeth with false passes or counterfeit writings
§ Numans, Newgate Market
¶ Nigling, company keeping with a woman: this word is not vsed now, but *wapping*, and thereof comes the name *wapping morts*, whoores.
§ To plant, to hide
¶ Smellar, a garden; not smelling cheate, for that 's a Nosegay
§ Spreader, butter
§ Whittington, Newgate.

"And thus haue I runne ouer the Canter's Dictionary; to speake more at large would aske more time then I haue allotted me; yet in this short time that I haue, I meane to sing song for song with the Belman, ere I wholly leaue him." [Here follow three Canting Songs.] Sign. E 1, back—E 4.

"And thus hath the Belman, through his pitifull ambition, caused me to write that I would not: And whereas he disclaims the name of Brotherhood, I here vtterly renounce him & his fellowship, as not desirous to be resolued of anything he professeth on this subiect, knowing my selfe to be as fully instructed herein as euer he was."—Sign. F.

In the second Part of his *Belman of London*, namely, his *Lanthorne and Candle-light*, 1609, Dekker printed a Dictionary of Canting, which is only a reprint of Harman's (p. 82-4, below). A few extracts from this *Lanthorne* are subjoined:

Canting.

"This word *canting* seemes to bee deriued from the latine *verbe canto*, which signifies in English, to sing, or to make a sound with words,—that is to say, to speake. And very aptly may *canting* take his deriuation, *a cantando*, from singing, because, amongst these beggerly consorts that can play vpon no better instruments, the language of *canting* is a kind of musicke; and he that in such assemblies can *cant* best, is counted the best Musitian."—*Dekker's Lanthorne and Candle-light*, B. 4. back.

Specimen of "Canting rithmes."

" Enough—with bowsy Coue maund Nace,
Tour the Patring Coue in the Darkeman Case,
Docked the Dell, for a Coper meke
His wach shall feng a Prounces Nab-chete,
Cyarum, by Salmon, and thou shalt pek my Iere
In thy Gan, for my watch it is nace gere,
For the bene bowse my watch hath a win, &c."

Dekker's Lanthorne, &c., C. 1. back.

A specimen of "Canting prose," with translation, is given on the same page.

Dekker's dictionary of Canting, given in *Lanthorne and Candle-light*, is the same as that of Harman.

" A Canting Song.

The Ruffin cly the nab of the Harman beck,
If we mawn'd Pannam, lap or Ruff-peck,
Or poplars of yarum : he cuts, bing to the Ruffmans,
Or els he sweares by the light-mans,
To put our stamps in the Harmans,
The ruffian cly the ghost of the Harman beck
If we heaue a booth we cly the Ierke.
If we niggle, or mill a bowsing Ken
Or nip a boung that has but a win
Or dup the giger of a Gentry cofe's ken,
To the quier cuffing we bing,
And then to the quier Ken, to scowre the Cramp ring,
And then to the Trin'de on the chates, in the lightmans
The Bube *and* Ruffian cly the Harman beck *and* harmans

Thus Englished.

The Diuell take the Constable's head,
If we beg Bacon, Butter-milke, or bread,
Or Pottage, to the hedge he bids vs hie
Or sweares (by this light) i' th' stocks we shall lie.
The Deuill haunt the Constable's ghoast
If we rob but a Booth, we are whip'd at a poast.
If an ale-house we rob, or be tane with a whore,
Or cut a purse that has inst a penny, and no more,
Or come but stealing in at a Gentleman's dore
To the Iustice straight we goe,
And then to the Iayle to be shakled : And so

> To be hang'd on the gallowes i' th' day time: the pox
> And the Deuill take the Constable and his stocks."
>
> *Ibid.* C. 3. back.

Richard Head (says Mr Hotten), in his *English Rogue, described in the Life of Meriton Latroon, a Witty Extravagant*, 4 vols. 12mo., 1671-80, gave " a glossary of Cant words 'used by the Gipsies'; but it was only a reprint of what Decker had given sixty years before," and therefore merely taken from Harman too. 'The Bibliography of Slang, Cant, and Vulgar Language' has been given so fully at the end of Mr Hotten's Slang Dictionary, that I excuse myself from pursuing the subject farther. I only add here Mr Wood's extracts from four of the treatises on this subject not noticed by Mr Hotten in the 1864 edition of his Dictionary, but contained (with others) in a most curious volume in the British Museum, labelled *Practice of Robbers*,—Press Mark 518. h. 2.,—as also some of the slang words in these little books not given by Harman [1]:

1. *The Catterpillers of this Nation anatomized, in a brief yet notable Discovery of House-breakers, Pick-pockets, &c. Together with the Life of a penitent High-way-man, discovering the Mystery of that Infernal Society. To which is added, the Manner of Hectoring and trapanning, as it is acted in and about the City of London. London, Printed for M. H. at the Princes Armes, in Chancery-lane.* 1659.

 Ken = miller, house-breaker
 lowre, or mint = wealth or money
 Gigers jacked = locked doors
 Tilers, or Cloyers, equivalent to shoplifters
 Joseph, a cloak
 Bung-nibber, or Cutpurse = a pickpocket.

---

2. *A Warning for Housekeepers; or, A discovery of all sorts of thieves and Robbers which go under theee titles, viz.—The Gilter, the Mill, the Glasier, Budg and Snudg, File-lifter, Tongue-padder, The private Theif. With Directions how to prevent them, Also an exact description of every one of their Practices. Written by one who was a Prisoner in Newgate. Printed for T. Newton*, 1676.

Glasiers, thieves who enter houses, thro' windows, first remouing a pane of glass (p. 4).

---

[1] We quote from four out of the five tracts contained in the volume. The title of the tract we do not quote is '*Hanging not Punishment enough*,' etc., London, 1701.

The following is a Budg and Snudg song :—
> "The Budge it is a delicate trade,
> And a delicate trade of fame ;
> For when that we have bit the bloe,
> We carry away the game :
> But if the cully nap us,
> And the lurres from us take,
> O then they rub us to the whitt,
> And it is hardly worth a make.
> But when that we come to the whitt
> Our Darbies to behold,
> And for to take our penitency,
> And boose the water cold.
> But when that we come out agen,
> As we walk along the street,
> We bite the Culley of his cole,
> But we are rubbed unto the whitt.
> And when that we come to the whitt,
> For garnish they do cry,
> Mary, faugh, you son of a wh——
> Ye shall have it by and by.
> But when that we come to **Tyburn**,
> For going upon the budge,
> There stands Jack Catch, that son of a w——
> That owes us all a grudge
> And when that he hath noosed us
> And our friends tips him no cole
> O then he throws us in the cart
> And tumbles us into the hole."—(pp. 5, 6.)

On the last page of this short tract (which consists of eight pages) we are promised :

"In the next Part you shall have a fuller description."

---

3. *Street Robberies consider'd ; The reason of their being so frequent, with probable means to prevent 'em : To which is added three short Treatises*—1. *A Warning for Travellers ;* 2. *Observations on Housebreakers ;* 3. *A Caveat for Shopkeepers.* London, J. Roberts. [no date] *Written by a converted Thief.*

Shepherd is mentioned in this book as being a clever prison breaker (p. 6). There is a long list of slang words in this tract. The following are only a few of them :

Abram, Naked
Betty, a Picklock
Bubble-Buff, Bailiff
Bube, Pox
Chive, a Knife
Clapper dudgeon, a beggar born
Collar the Cole, Lay hold on the money

Cull, a silly fellow
Dads, an old man
Darbies, Iron
Diddle, Geneva
Earnest, share
Elf, little
Fencer, receiver of stolen goods
Fib, to beat
Fog, smoke
Gage, Exciseman
Gilt, a Picklock
Grub, Provender
Hic, booby
Hog, a shilling
Hum, strong
Jem, Ring
Jet, Lawyer
Kick, Sixpence
Kin, a thief
Kit, Dancing-master
Lap, Spoon-meat
Latch, let in
Leake, Welshman
Leap, all safe
Mauks, a whore
Mill, to beat
Mish, a smock
Mundungus, sad stuff
Nan, a maid of the house
Nap, an arrest
Nimmiug, stealing
Oss Chives, Bone-handled knives
Otter, a sailor
Peter, Portmantua
Plant the Whids, take care what you say
Popps, Pistols
Rubbs, hard shifts
Rumbo Ken, Pawn-brokers
Rum Mort, fine Woman
Smable, taken
Smeer, a painter
Snafflers, Highwaymen
Snic, to cut
Tattle, watch
Tic, trust
Tip, give
Tit, a horse
Tom Pat, a parson
Tout, take heed
Tripe, the belly
Web, cloth
Wobble, 'o boil
Yam, to eat
Yelp, a crier
Yest, a day ago
Zad, crooked
Znees, Frost
Zouch, an ungenteel man
&c., a Bookseller

"The King of the Night, as the Constables please to term themselves, should be a little more active in their employment; but all their business is to get to a watch house and guzzle, till their time of going home comes." (p. 60.)

"A small bell to Window Shutters would be of admirable use to prevent Housebreakers." (p. 70.)

4. *A true discovery of the Conduct of Receivers and Thief-Takers, in and about the City of London,* &c., &c. London, 1718.

This pamphlet is "design'd as preparatory to a larger Treatise, wherein shall be propos'd Methods to extirpate and suppress for the future such villanous Practices." It is by "Charles Hitchin, one of the Marshals of the City of London."

I now take leave of Harman, with a warm commendation of him to the reader.

The third piece in the present volume is a larky Sermon in praise of Thieves and Thievery, the title of which (p. 93, below) happened to catch my eye when I was turning over the Cotton Catalogue, and which was printed here, as well from its suiting the subject, as from a pleasant recollection of a gallop some 30 years ago in a four-horse coach across Harford-Bridge-Flat, where Parson Haben (or Hyberdyne), who is said to have preached the Sermon, was no doubt robbed. My respected friend Goody-goody declares the sermon to be 'dreadfully irreverent;' but one needn't mind him. An earlier copy than the Cotton one turned up among the Lansdowne MSS, and as it differed a good deal from the Cotton text, it has been printed opposite to that.

Of the fourth piece in this little volume, *The Groundworke of Conny-catching*, less its reprint from Harman, I have spoken above, at p. xiv. There was no good in printing the whole of it, as we should then have had Harman twice over.

The growth of the present Text was on this wise: Mr Viles suggested a reprint of Stace's reprint of Harman in 1573, after it had been read with the original, and collated with the earlier editions. The first edition I could not find, but ascertained, with some trouble, and through Mr H. C. Hazlitt, where the second and third editions were, and borrowed the 3rd of its ever-generous owner, Mr Henry Huth. Then Mr Hazlitt told me of Awdeley, which he thought was borrowed from Harman. However, Harman's own words soon settled that point; and Awdeley had to precede Harman. Then the real bagger from Harman, the *Groundworke*, had to be added, after the Parson's Sermon. Mr Viles read the proofs and revises of Harman with the original: Mr Wood and I have made the Index; and I, because Mr Viles is more desperately busy than myself, have written the Preface.

The extracts from Mr J. P. Collier must be taken for what they are worth. I have not had time to verify them; but assume them to be correct, and not ingeniously or unreasonably altered from their originals, like Mr Collier's print of Henslowe's Memorial, of which

Dr Ingleby complains,[1] and like his notorious Alleyn letter. If some one only would follow Mr Collier through all his work—pending his hoped-for Retractations,—and assure us that the two pieces above-named, and the Perkins Folio, are the only things we need reject, such some-one would render a great service to all literary antiquarians, and enable them to do justice to the wonderful diligence, knowledge, and acumen, of the veteran pioneer in their path. Certainly, in most of the small finds which we workers at this Text thought we had made, we afterwards found we had been anticipated by Mr Collier's *Registers of the Stationers' Company*, or *Bibliographical Catalogue*, and that the facts were there rightly stated.

[1] To obviate the possibility of mistake in the lection of this curious document, Mr E. W. Ashbee has, at my request, and by permission of the Governors of Dulwich College (where the paper is preserved), furnished me with an exact fac-simile of it, worked off on somewhat similar paper. By means of this fac-simile my readers may readily assure themselves that in no part of the memorial is Lodge called a "player;" indeed he is not called "Thos. Lodge," and it is only an inference, an unavoidable conclusion, that the Lodge here spoken of is Thomas Lodge, the dramatist. Mr Collier, however, professes to find that he is there called "Thos. Lodge," and that it [the Memorial] contains this remarkable grammatical inversion;

"and haveinge some knowledge and acquaintaunce of him as a player, requested me to be his baile,"

which is evidently intended to mean, *as I had some knowledge and acquaintance of Lodge as a player, he requested me to be his baile.* But in this place the original paper reads thus,

"and havinge of me some knowledge and acquaintaunce requested me to be his bayle,"

meaning, of course, *Lodge, having some knowledge and acquaintance of me, requested me to be his bail.*

The interpolation of the five words needed to corroborate Mr Collier's explanation of the misquoted passage from Gosson, and the omission of two other words inconsistent with that interpolation, may be thought to exhibit some little ingenuity; it was, however, a feat which could have cost him no great pains. But the labour of recasting the orthography of the memorial must have been considerable; while it is difficult to imagine a rational motive to account for such labour being incurred. To expand the abbreviations and modernize the orthography might have been expedient, as it would have been easy. But, in the name of reason, what is the gain of writing *wheare* and *theare* for "where" and "there;" *cleere*, *yeeld*, and *meerly* for "clere," "yealde," and "merely;" *verie*, *anie*, *laie*, *waie*, *paie*, *yssue*, and *pryvily*, for "very," "any," "lay," "way," "pay," "issue," and "privylie;" *sondrie*, *begon*, and *doen* for "sundrie," "began," and "don;" and *thintent*, *thaction*, and *thacceptaunce* for "the intent," "the action," and "the acceptaunce"?—p. 14 of Dr C. M. Ingleby's '*Was Thomas Lodge an Actor? An Exposition touching the Social Status of the Playwright in the time of Queen Elizabeth.*' Printed for the Author by R. Barrett and Sons, 13 Mark Lane, 1868. 2s. 6d.

That there is pure metal in Mr Collier's work, and a good deal of it, few will doubt; but the dross needs refining out. I hope that the first step in the process may be the printing of the whole of the Stationers' Registers from their start to 1700 at least, by the Camden Society,—within whose range this work well lies,—or by the new Harleian or some other Society. It ought not to be left to the 'Early English Text' to do some 20 years hence.

F. J. FURNIVALL.

29 *Nov.*, 1869.

P.S. For a curious Ballad describing beggars' tricks in the 17th century, say about 1650, see the Roxburghe Collection, i. 42-3, and the Ballad Society's reprint, now in the press for 1869, i. 137-41, '*The cunning Northerne Beggar*': 1. he shams lame; 2. he pretends to be a poor soldier; 3. a sailor; 4. cripple; 5. diseased; 6. festered all over, and face daubed with blood; 7. blind; 8. has had his house burnt.

NOTES.

p. vii. ix, p. 19, 20. *Elizabeth, Countess of Shrewsbury, and her parish.* The manor of Erith was granted to Elizabeth, Countess of Shrewsbury, by Henry VIII. in the 36th year of his reign, A.D. 1544-5. The Countess died in 1567, and was buried in the parish church of Erith. "The manor of Eryth becoming part of the royal revenue, continued in the crown till K. Henry VIII. in his 36th year, granted it in fee to Elizabeth, relict of George, Earl of Shrewsbury, by the description of the *manor, of Eryth, alias Lysnes,* with all its members and appurts., and also all that wood, called Somersden, lying in Eryth, containing 30 acres; and a wood, called Ludwood, there, containing 50 acres; and a wood, called Fridayes-hole, by estimation, 20 acres, to hold of the King *in capite* by knight's service.[1] She was the second wife of George, Earl of Shrews-

---

[1] Rot. Esch. ejus an, pt. 6.

bury, Knight of the Garter,[1] who died July 26, anno 33 K. Henry VIII.,[2] by whom she had issue one son, John, who died young; and Anne, married to Peter Compton, son and heir of Sir Wm. Compton, Knt., who died in the 35th year of K. Henry VIII., under age, as will be mentioned hereafter. Elizabeth, Countess of Shrewsbury, in Easter Term, in the 4th year of Q. Elizabeth, levied a fine of this manor, with the passage over the Thames; and dying in the tenth year of that reign, anno 1567,[3] lies buried under a sumptuous tomb, in this church. Before her death this manor, &c., seem to have been settled on her only daughter Anne, then wife of Wm. Herbert, Earl of Pembroke, and widow of Peter Compton, as before related, who was in possession of it, with the passage over the Thames, anno 9 Q. Elizabeth."—Hasted's *History of Kent*, vol. i. p. 196.

p. ix. In Lambarde's *Perambulation of Kent* (edit. 1826), p. 66, he mentions " Thomas Harman " as being one of the " Kentish writers."

Lambarde, in the same volume, p. 60, also mentions " Abacuk Harman " as being the name of one " of suche of the nobilitie and gentrie, as the Heralds recorded in their visitation in 1574."

There is nothing about Harman in Mr Sandys's book on Gavelkind, &c., *Consuetudines Cantiæ*. To future inquirers perhaps the following book may be of use:

" *Bibliotheca Cantiana*: A Bibliographical Account of what has been published on the History, Topography, Antiquities, Customs, and Family History of the County of Kent." By John Russell Smith.

p. 1, 12. *The xxv. Orders of Knaues.*—Mr Collier gives an entry in the Stationers' Registers in 1585-6: " Edward White. Rd. of him, for printinge xxij^{ti} ballades at iiij^d a peece—vij^s iiij^d, and xiiij. more at ij^d a peece ij^s iiij^d . . . . ix^s viij^d" And No. 23 is " The xxv^{tie} orders of knaves."—*Stat. Reg.* ii. 207.

p. 22. *The last Duke of Buckingham was beheaded.*—Edward Stafford, third Duke of Buckingham, one of Henry VIII's and Wolsey's victims, was beheaded on Tower Hill, May 17, 1521, for 'imagining' the king's death. ('The murnynge of Edward Duke of Buckyngham' was one of certain 'ballettes' licensed to Mr John Wallye and Mrs Toye in 1557-8, says Mr J. P. Collier, *Stat. Reg.* i. 4.) His father (Henry Stafford) before him suffered the same fate in 1483, having been betrayed by his servant Bannister after his unsuccessful rising in Brecon.—*Percy Folio Ballads*, ii. 253.

---

[1] This lady was one of the daughters and co-heirs of Sir Richard Walden, of this parish, Knt., and the Lady Margaret his wife, who both lie buried in this church [of Erith]. He was, as I take it, made Knight of the Bath in the 17th year of K. Henry VII., his estate being then certified to be 40*l.* per annum, being the son of Richard Walden, esq. Sir Richard and Elizabeth his wife both lie buried here. *MSS. Dering.*

[2] Dugd. Bar. vol. i. p. 332.

[3] Harman's dedication of his book to her was no doubt written in 1566, and his 2nd edition, in both states, published before the Countess's death.

p. 23. *Egiptians.* The Statute 22 Hen. VIII. c. 10 is *An Acte concernyny Egypsyans.* After enumerating the frauds committed by the "outlandysshe people callynge themselfes Egyptians," the first section provides that they shall be punished by Imprisonment and loss of goods, and be deprived of the benefit of 8 Hen. VI. c. 29. "de medietate linguæ." The second section is a proclamation for the departure from the realm of all such Egyptians. The third provides that stolen goods shall be restored to their owners; and the fourth, that one moiety of the goods seized from the Egyptians shall be given to the seizer.

p. 48, l. 5. *The Lord Sturtons man; and when he was executed.* Charles Stourton, 7th Baron, 1548—1557:—" Which Charles, with the help of four of his own servants in his own house, committed a shameful murther upon one Hargill, and his son, with whom he had been long at variance, and buried their Carcasses 50 foot deep in the earth, thinking thereby to prevent the discovery; but it coming afterwards to light, he had sentence of death passed upon him, which he suffer'd at Salisbury, the 6th of March, Anno 1557, 4 Phil. & Mary, by an Halter of Silk, in respect of his quality."—*The Peerage of England*, vol. ii. p. 24 (Lond., 1710).

p. 77. *Saint Quinten's.* Saint Quinten was invoked against coughs, says Brand, ed. Ellis, 1841, i. 196.

p. 77. *The Three Cranes in the Vintry.* "Then the Three Cranes' lane, so called, not only of *a sign of three cranes at a tavern door*, but rather of three strong cranes of timber placed on the Vintry wharf by the Thames side, to crane up wines there, as is afore showed. This lane was of old time, to wit, the 9th of Richard II., called The Painted Tavern lane, of the tavern being painted."—Stow's *Survey of London*, ed. by Thoms, p. 90.

"The Three Cranes was formerly a favourite London sign. With the usual jocularity of our forefathers, an opportunity for punning could not be passed; so, instead of the three cranes, which in the vintry used to lift the barrels of wine, three birds were represented. The Three Cranes in Thames Street, or in the vicinity, was a famous tavern as early as the reign of James I. It was one of the taverns frequented by the wits in Ben Jonson's time. In one of his plays he says:—

'A pox o' these pretenders! to wit, your *Three Cranes*, Mitre and Mermaid men! not a corn of true salt, not a grain of right mustard among them all!'—*Bartholomew Fair*, act i. sc. 1.

"On the 23rd of January, 166½ Pepys suffered a strong mortification of the flesh in having to dine at this tavern with some poor relations. The sufferings of the snobbish secretary must have been intense:—

'By invitation to my uncle Fenner's, and where I found his new wife, a *pitiful, old, ugly, ill-bred* woman in a hatt, a mid-wife. Here were many of his, and as many of her, relations, *sorry, mean people;* and after choosing our gloves, we all went over to the Three Cranes Taverne:

and though the best room of the house, in such a narrow dogghole we were crammed, and I believe we were near 40, that it made me loath my company and victuals, and a very poor dinner it was too.'

"Opposite this tavern people generally left their boats to shoot the bridge, walking round to Billingsgate, where they would reenter them."—Hotten's *History of Signboards*, p. 204.

p. 77. *Saynt Iulyans in Thystellworth parish.* 'Thistleworth, see Isleworth,' says Walker's Gazetteer, ed. 1801. That there might well have been a St Julyan's Inn there we learn from the following extract:

"St. Julian, the patron of travellers, wandering minstrels, boatmen,[1] &c., was a very common inn sign, because he was supposed to provide good lodgings for such persons. Hence two St Julian's crosses, in saltier, are in chief of the innholders' arms, and the old motto was:— 'When I was harbourless, ye lodged me.' This benevolent attention to travellers procured him the epithet of 'the good herbergeor,' and in France '*bon herbet.*' His legend in a MS., Bodleian, 1596, fol. 4, alludes to this:—

'Therfore yet to this day, thei that over lond wende,
They biddeth Seint Julian, anon, that gode herborw he hem sende;
And Seint Julianes Pater Noster ofte seggeth also
For his faders soule, and his moderes, that he hem bring therto.'

And in '*Le dit des Heureux,*' an old French fabliau:—

'Tu as dit la patenotre
Saint Julian à cest matin,
Soit en Roumans, soit en Latin;
Or tu seras bien ostilé.'

In mediæval French, *L'hotel Saint Julien* was synonymous with good cheer.

'—— Sommes tuit vostre.
Par Saint Pierre le bon Apostre,
L'ostel aurez Saint Julien,'

says Mabile to her feigned uncle in the fabliau of '*Boivin de Provins;*' and a similar idea appears in 'Cocke Lorell's bote,' where the crew, after the entertainment with the 'relygyous women' from the Stews' Bank, at Colman's Hatch,

'Blessyd theyr shyppe when they had done,
And dranke about a *Saint Julyan's* tonne.'
Hotten's *History of Signboards,*" p. 283.

"Isleworth in Queen Elizabeth's time was commonly in conversation,

[1] Of pilgrims, and of whoremongers, say Brand and Sir H. Ellis (referring to the *Hist. des Troubadours*, tom. i. p. 11,) in *Brand's Antiquities*, ed. 1841, i. 202. Chaucer makes him the patron of hospitality, saying of the Frankeleyn, in the Prologue to the *Canterbury Tales*, "Seynt Iulian he was in his contre." Mr Hazlitt, in his new edition of Brand, i. 303, notes that as early as the *Ancren Riwle*, ab. 1220 A.D., we have 'Surely they (the pilgrims) find St. Julian's inn, which wayfaring men diligently seek.'

and sometimes in records, called Thistleworth."—Lysons' *Environs of London*, vol. iii. p. 79.

p. 77. *Rothered:* ? Rotherhithe.

p. 77. *The Kynges Barne,* betwene Detforde and Rothered, can hardly be the great hall of Eltham palace. Lysons (*Environs of London*, iv. p. 399) in 1796, says the hall was then used as a barn ; and in vol. vi. of the *Archæologia*, p. 367, it is called " King John's Barn."

p. 77. *Ketbroke.* Kidbrooke is marked in large letters on the east of Blackheath on the mordern Ordnance-map ; and on the road from Blackheath to Eltham are the villages or hamlets of Upper Kidbrooke and Lower Kidbrooke.

" Kedbrooke lies adjoining to Charlton, on the south side of the London Road, a small distance from Blackheath. It was antiently written Cicebroc, and was once a parish of itself, though now (1778 A.D.) it is esteemed as an appendage to that of Charlton."—Hasted's *History of Kent*, vol. i. p. 40.

p. 100. *Sturbridge Fair.* Stourbridge, or Sturbich, the name of a common field, extending between Chesterton and Cambridge, near the little brook Sture, for about half a mile square, is noted for its fair, which is kept annually on September 19th, and continues a fortnight. It is surpassed by few fairs in Great Britain, or even in Europe, for traffic, though of late it is much lessened. The booths are placed in rows like streets, by the name[s] of which they are called, as Cheapside, &c., and are filled with all sorts of trades. The Duddery, an area of 80 or 100 yards square, resembles Blackwell Hall. Large commissions are negotiated here for all parts of England in *cheese*, woolen goods, wool, leather, hops, upholsterers' and ironmongers' ware, &c. &c. Sometimes 50 hackney coaches from London, ply morning and night, to and from Cambridge, as well as all the towns round, and the very barns and stables are turned into inns for the accommodation of the poorer people. After the wholesale business is over, the country gentry generally flock in, laying out their money in stage-plays, taverns, music-houses, toys, puppet-shows, &c., and the whole concludes with a day for the sale of horses. This fair is under the jurisdiction of the University of Cambridge.—*Walker's Gazetteer*, ed. 1801. See Index to Brand's *Antiquities*.

THE
Fraternitye of Vacabondes.

As wel of ruflyng Vacabondes, as of beggerly, of women as of men, of Gyrles as of Boyes,

with

their proper names and qualities.

With a description of the crafty company of

Cousoners and Shifters.

¶ Wherunto also is adioyned

the .xxv. Orders of Knaues,

otherwyse called

a Quartern of Knaues.

Confirmed for euer by Cocke Lorell.

(✶)

¶ **The Vprightman speaketh.**
¶ Our Brotherhood[1] of Vacabondes,
   If you would know where dwell:
   In graues end Barge which syldome standes,
   The talke wyll shew ryght well.

¶ **Cocke Lorell aunswereth.**
¶ Some orders of my Knaues also
   In that Barge shall ye fynde:
   For no where shall ye walke I trow,
   But ye shall see their kynde.

¶ Imprinted at London by Iohn Awdeley, dwellyng in little
Britayne streete without Aldersgate.
1575.

[1] *Orig.* Brothethood.

[leaf 1 b.] ¶ *The Printer to the Reader.*

THis brotherhood of Vacabondes,
 To shew that there be such in deede ·
Both Iustices and men of Landes,
Wyll testifye it if it neede.
  For at a Sessions as they sat,
   By chaunce a Vacabond was got.

¶ Who promysde if they would him spare,
And keepe his name from knowledge then:
He would as straunge a thing declare,
As euer they knew synce they were men.
  But if my fellowes do know (sayd he)
   That thus I dyd, they would kyll me.

¶ They graunting him this his request,
He dyd declare as here is read,
Both names and states of most and least,
Of this their Vacabondes brotherhood.
  Which at the request of a worshipful ma*n*
  I haue set it forth as well as I can.

FINIS.

[leaf 2]

¶ The
Fraternitye of Vacabondes

both rufling and beggerly,

Men and women, Boyes and Gyrles,

wyth

their proper names and qualities.

Whereunto are adioyned

the company of Cousoners and Shifters.

¶ AN ABRAHAM MAN.

AN Abraham man is he that walketh bare armed, and bare legged, and fayneth hym selfe mad, and caryeth a packe of wool, or a stycke with baken on it, or such lyke toy, and nameth himselfe poore Tom.

¶ A RUFFELER.

A Ruffeler goeth wyth a weapon to seeke seruice, saying he hath bene a Seruitor in the wars, and beggeth for his reliefe. But his chiefest trade is to robbe poore wayfaring men and market women.

¶ A PRYGMAN.

A Prygman goeth with a stycke in hys hand like an idle person. His propertye is to steale cloathes of the hedge, which they call storing of the Rogeman: or els filtch Poultry, carying them to the Alehouse, whych they call the Bowsyng In, & ther syt playing at cardes and dice, tyl that is spent which they haue so fylched.

¶ A WHIPIACKE.

A Whypiacke is one, that by coulor of a counterfaite Lisence (which they call a Gybe, and the scales they cal Iarckes) doth vse to beg lyke a Maryner, But hys chiefest trade is to rob Bowthes in a Faire, or to pilfer ware from staules, which they cal heauing of the Bowth.

¶ A FRATER.

A Frater goeth wyth a like Lisence to beg for some Spittlehouse or Hospital. Their pray is commonly vpon [leaf 2 b.] poore women as they go and come to the Markets.

¶ A QUIRE BIRD.

A Quire bird is one that came lately out of prison, & goeth to seeke seruice. He is commonly a stealer of Horses, which they terme a Priggar of Paulfreys.

¶ AN VPRIGHT MAN.

An Vpright man is one that goeth wyth the trunchion of a staffe, which staffe they cal a Filtchman. This man is of so much authority, that meeting with any of his profession, he may cal them to accompt, & commaund a share or snap vnto him selfe, of al that they haue gained by their trade in one moneth. And if he doo them wrong, they haue no remedy agaynst hym, no though he beate them, as he vseth commonly to do. He may also commaund any of their women, which they cal Doxies, to serue his turne. He hath ye chiefe place at any market walke, & other assembles, & is not of any to be controled.

¶ A CURTALL.

A Curtall is much like to the Vpright man, but hys authority is not fully so great. He vseth commonly to go with a short cloke, like to grey Friers, & his woman with him in like liuery, which he calleth his Altham if she be hys wyfe, & if she be his harlot, she is called hys Doxy.

¶ A PALLIARD.

A Palliard is he that goeth in a patched cloke, and hys Doxy goeth in like apparell.

¶ AN IRISHE TOYLE.

An Irishe toyle is he that carieth his ware in hys wallet, as laces, pins, poyntes, and such like. He vseth to shew no wares vntill he haue his almes. And if the good man and wyfe be not in the way, he procureth of the ch[i]ldre*n* or seruants a fleece of wool, or the worth of xij.d. of some other thing, for a peniworth of his wares.

[leaf 3.]

¶ A IACK MAN.

A Iackeman is he that can write and reade, and somtime speake latin. He vseth to make counterfaite licences which they call Gybes, and sets to Seales, in their language called Iarkes.

¶ A SWYGMAN.

A Swygman goeth with a Pedlers pack.

¶ A WASHMAN.

A Washman is called a Palliard, but not of the right making. He vseth to lye in the hye way with lame or sore legs or armes to beg. These me*n* ye right Pilliards wil often times spoile, but they dare not complayn. They be bitten with Spickworts, & somtime with rats bane.

¶ A TINKARD.

A Tinkard leaueth his bag a sweating at the Alehouse, which they terme their Bowsing In, and in the meane season goeth abrode a begging.

¶ A WYLDE ROGE.

A wilde Roge is he that hath no abiding place but by his coulour of going abrode to beg, is commonly to seeke some kinsman of his, and all that be of hys corporation be properly called Roges.

¶ A KITCHEN CO.

A Kitchin Co is called an ydle runagate Boy.

¶ A KITCHEN MORTES.

A Kitchin Mortes is a Gyrle, she is brought at her full age to the Vpryght man to be broken, and so she is called a Doxy, vntil she come to ye honor of an Altham.

¶ DOXIES.

Note especially all which go abroade working laces and shirt stringes, they name them Doxies.

¶ A PATRIARKE CO.

A Patriarke Co doth make mariages, & that is vntill [leaf 3 b.] death depart the maried folke, which is after this sort: When they come to a dead Horse or any dead Catell, then they shake hands and so depart euery one of them a seuerall way

---

¶ THE COMPANY OF COUSONERS AND SHIFTERS.

¶ A CURTESY MAN.

A Curtesy man is one that walketh about the back lanes in London in the day time, and sometime in the broade streetes in the night season, and when he meeteth some handsome yong man clenly apareled, or some other honest Citizen, he maketh humble salutations and low curtesy, and sheweth him that he hath a worde or two to speake with his mastership. This child can behaue him selfe manerly, for he wyll desire him that he talketh withall, to take the vpper hand, and shew him much reuerence, and at last like his familier acquaintaunce will put on his cap, and walke syde by syde, and talke on this fashion: Oh syr, you seeme to be a man, and one that fauoureth men, and therefore I am the more bolder to breake my mind vnto your good maistership. Thus it is syr, ther is a certaine of vs (though I say it both taule and handsome men of theyr hands) which haue come lately from the wars, and as God knoweth haue nothing to take to, being both maisterles and moniles, & knowing no way wherby to yerne one peny. And further, wher as we haue bene welthely brought vp, and we also haue beene had in good estimation, we are a shamed now to declare our misery, and to fall a crauing as common Beggers, and as for to steale and robbe, (God is our record) it striketh vs to [leaf 4] the hart, to thinke of such a mischiefe, that euer any handsome man should fall into such a daunger for thys worldly trash. Which if we had to suffise our want and necessity, we should neuer seeke thus shamefastly to craue on such good pityfull men as you seeme to be, neither yet so daungerously to hasarde our liues for so vyle a thing. Therefore good syr, as you seeme to be a handsome man your selfe, and also such a one as pitieth the miserable case of handsome men, as now your eyes and countenaunce sheweth to haue some pity vppon this my miserable complainte : So in Gods cause I require your maistershyp, & in the behalfe of my poore afflicted fellowes, which though here in sight they cry not with me to you, yet wheresouer they bee, I am sure they cry vnto God to moue the heartes of some good men to shew forth their liberality in this behalfe. All which & I with them craue now the same request at your good masterships hand. With these or such like words he frameth his talke. Now if the party (which he thus talketh withall) profereth hym a peny or .ii.d. he taketh it, but verye scornfully, and at last speaketh on this sorte : Well syr, your good will is not to be refused. But yet you shall vnderstand (good syr) that this is nothing for them, for whom I do thus shamefastly entreate. Alas syr, it is not a groate or .xii.d. I speake for, being such a company of Seruiters as wee haue bene : yet neuertheles God forbid I should not receiue your ge*n*tle offer at this time, hoping hereafter through your good motions to some such lyke good gentleman as you be, that I, or some of my fellowes in my place, shall finde the more liberality. These kind of ydle Vacabondes wyll go commonly well appareled, without [leaf 4 b.] any weapon, and in place where they meete together, as at their hosteryes or other places, they wyll beare the port of ryght good gentlemen, & some are the more trusted, but co*m*monly thei pay them w*ith* stealing a paire of sheetes, or Couerlet, & so take their farewell earely in the morning, before the mayster or dame be sturring.

¶ A CHEATOUR OR FINGERER.

These commonly be such kinde of idle Vacabondes as scarcely a man shall discerne, they go so gorgeously, sometime with waiting men, and sometime without. Their trade is to walke in such places, where as gentelmen & other worshipfull Citizens do resorte, as at

Poules, or at Christes Hospital, & somtime at ye Royal exchaunge. These haue very many acquaintaunces, yea, and for the most part will acquaint them selues with euery man, and fayne a society, in one place or other. But chiefly they wil seeke their acquaintaunce of such (which they haue learned by diligent enquiring where they resort) as haue receyued some porcioun of money of their friends, as yong Gentlemen which are sent to London to study the lawes, or els some yong Marchant man or other kynde of Occupier, whose friendes hath geuen them a stock of mony[1] to occupy withall. When they haue thus found out such a pray, they will find the meanes by theyr familiarity, as very curteously to bid him to breakefast at one place or other, where they are best acquainted, and closely amonge themselues wil appoint one of their Fraternity, which they call a Fyngerer, an olde beaten childe, not onely in such deceites, but also such a one as by his age is painted out with gray heares, wrinkled face, crooked back, and most commonly lame, as it might seeme with age, [leaf 5] yea and such a one as to shew a simplicity, shal weare a homely cloke and hat scarce worth .vi. d. This nimble fingred knight (being appointed to this place) commeth in as one not knowen of these Cheatours, but as vnwares shal sit down at the end of the bord where they syt, & call for his peny pot of wine, or a pinte of Ale, as the place serueth. Thus sitting as it were alone, mumblyng on a crust, or some such thing, these other yonckers wil finde some kind of mery talke with him, some times questioning wher he dwelleth, & sometimes enquiring what trade he vseth, which commonly he telleth them he vseth husbandry : & talking thus merely, at last they aske him, how sayest thou, Father, wylt thou play for thy breakfast with one of vs, that we may haue some pastime as we syt ? Thys olde Karle makyng it straunge at the first saith : My maysters, ich am an old man, and halfe blinde, and can skyl of very few games, yet for that you seeme to be such good Gentelmen, as to profer to play for that of which you had no part, but onely I my selfe, and therefore of right ich am worthy to pay for it, I shal with al my hart fulfyl your request. And so falleth to play, somtime at Cardes, & sometime at dice. Which through his counterfait simplicity

---

[1] *Orig.* mony

in the play somtimes ouer counteth himself, or playeth somtimes against his wyl, so as he would not, & then counterfaiteth to be angry, and falleth to swearing, & so leesing that, profereth to play for a shillyng or two. The other therat hauing good sport, seming to mocke him, falleth againe to play, and so by their legerdemane, & counterfaiting, winneth ech of them a shilling or twain, & at last whispereth the yong man in the eare to play with hym also, that ech one might haue a fling at him. [leaf 5 b.] This yong man for company falleth againe to play also with the sayd Fyngerer, and winneth as the other did which when he had loste a noble or .vi. s. maketh as though he had lost al his mony, and falleth a intreating for parte thereof againe to bring him home, which the other knowing his mind and intent, stoutely denieth and iesteth, & scoffeth at him. This Fingerer seeming then to be in a rage, desireth them as they are true gentlemen, to tarry till he fetcheth more store of money, or els to point some place where they may meete. They seeming greedy hereof, promiseth faithfully and clappeth handes so to meete. They thus ticklyng the young man in the eare, willeth him to make as much money as he can, and they wil make as much as they can, and consent as though they wil play booty against him. But in the ende they so vse the matter, that both the young man leeseth his part, and, as it seemeth to him, they leesing theirs also, and so maketh as though they would fal together by the eares with this fingerer, which by one wyle or other at last conueyeth him selfe away, & they as it were raging lyke mad bedlams, one runneth one way, an other an other way, leauing the loser indeede all alone. Thus these Cheatours at their accustomed hosteries meete closely together, and there receiue ech one his part of this their vile spoyle. Of this fraternity there be that be called helpers, which commonly haunt tauernes or alehouses, and commeth in as men not acquainted with none in the companye, but spying them at any game, wil byd them God spede and God be at their game, and will so place him selfe that he will shew his fellow by sygnes and tokens, without speech commonly, but sometime with far fetched [leaf 6] wordes, what cardes he hath in his hand, and how he may play against him. And those betwene them both getteth money out of the others purse.

¶ A RING FALLER.

A Ryng faller is he that getteth fayre copper rings, some made like signets, & some after other fashions, very faire gylded, & walketh vp and down the streetes, til he spieth some man of the country, or some other simple body whom he thinketh he may deceaue, and so goeth a lyttle before him or them, and letteth fall one of these ringes, which when the party that commeth after spieth and taketh it vp, he hauing an eye backward, crieth halfe part, the party that taketh it vp, thinking it to be of great value, profereth him some money for his part, which he not fully denieth, but willeth him to come into some alehouse or tauerne, and there they will common vpon the matter. Which when they come in, and are set in some solitary place (as commonly they call for such a place) there he desireth the party that found the ring to shew it him. When he seeth it, he falleth a entreating the party that found it, and desireth him to take money for his part, and telleth him that if euer he may do him any frendship hereafter he shal commaund him, for he maketh as though he were very desirous to haue it. The symple man seeing him so importune vpon it, thinketh the ring to bee of great valure, and so is the more lother to part from it. At last this ring faller asketh him what he will geue him for his part, for, saith he, seeing you wyl not let me haue the ring, alowe me my part, and take you the ring. The other asketh what he counteth the ring to be worth, he answereth, v. or vi. pound. No, saith he, it is not so much worth. [leaf 6 b.] Well (saith this Ringfaller) let me haue it, and I wyll alow you .xl. s. for your part. The other party standyng in a doubt, and looking on the ryng, asketh if he wyll geue the money out of hand. The other answereth, he hath not so much ready mony about him, but he wil go fetch so much for him, if he wil go with him. The other that found the ring, thinking he meaneth truly, beginneth to profer him .xx. s. for his part, sometymes more, or les, which he verye scornfullye refuseth at the first, and styl entreateth that he might haue the ring, which maketh the other more fonder of it, and desireth him to take the money for his part, & so profereth him money. This ring faller seing ye mony, maketh it very straunge, and first questioneth with him whor he dwelleth, and asketh him what is his name, & telleth him that he semeth to be an honest man, and therfore he wil do somwhat for friendships sake, hoping to haue as friendly a pleasure at his hand hereafter, and so profereth hym for .x. s. more he should haue the ryng. At last, with entreatye on both partes, he geueth the Ring faller the money, and so departeth, thinkyng he hath gotten a very great Iewell. These kynde of deceyuing Vacabondes haue other practises with their rings, as somtimes to come to buy wares of mens Prentesies, and sometimes of their Maisters, and when he hath agreed of the price, he sayth he hath not so much money about him, but pulleth of one of these rings of from his fyngers, and profereth to leaue it in pawne, tyl his Maister or his friendes hath sene it, so promising to bring the money, the seller thinking he meaneth truly, letteth him go, and neuer seeth him after, tyll perhaps at Tyburne or at such lyke place. Ther is another kinde of [leaf 7] these Ring choppers, which commonly cary about them a faire gold ring in deede, and these haue other counterfait rings made so lyke this gold ring, as ye shal not perceiue the contrary, tyl it be brought to ye touchstone. This child wyl come to borow mony of the right gold ring, the party mistrusting the Ring not to be good, goeth to the Goldsmith with the partye that hath the ryng, and tryeth it whether it be good golde, and also wayeth it to know how much it is worth. The Goldsmith tryeth it to be good gold, and also to haue hys ful weight like gold, and warenteth the party which shall lend the money that the ring is worth so much money according to the waight, this yoncker comming home with the party which shall lend the money, and hauing the gold ring againe, putteth vp the gold ring, and pulleth out a counterfaite ring very like the same, & so deliuereth it to the party which lendeth the money, they thinking it to be the same which they tryed, and so deliuereth the money or sometimes wares, and thus vily be deceiued.

¶ THE

.XXV. Orders of Knaues,

otherwise called

a quarterne of Knaues,

confirmed for euer by Cocke Lorell.

---

1 TROLL AND TROLL BY.

TRoll and Trol by, is he that setteth naught by no man, nor no man by him. This is he that would beare rule in a place, and hath none authority nor thanke, & at last is thrust out of the doore like a knaue.

2 TROLL WITH.

Troll with is he *that* no man shall know the seruaunt from ye Maister. This knaue with his cap on his head [leaf 7 b.] lyke Capon hardy, wyll syt downe by his Maister, or els go cheeke by cheeke with him in the streete.

3 TROLL HAZARD OF TRACE.

Troll hazard of trace is he that goeth behynde his Maister as far as he may see hym. Such knaues commonly vse to buy Spice-cakes, Apples, or other trifles, and doo eate them as they go in the streetes lyke vacabond Boyes.

4 TROLL HAZARD OF TRITRACE.

Troll hazard of tritrace, is he that goeth gaping after his Master, looking to and fro tyl he haue lost him. This knaue goeth gasyng about lyke a foole at euery toy, and then seeketh in euery house lyke a Maisterles dog, and when his Maister nedeth him, he is to seeke.

5 CHAFE LITTER.

Chafe Litter is he that wyll plucke vp the Fether-bed or Matrice, and pysse in the bedstraw, and wyl neuer ryse vncalled. This knaue berayeth many tymes in the corners of his Maisters chamber, or other places inconuenient, and maketh cleane hys shooes with the couerlet or curtaines.

6 OBLOQUIUM.

Obloquium is hee that wyll take a tale out of his Maisters mouth and tell it him selfe. He of right may be called a malapart knaue.

7 RINCE PYTCHER.

Rince Pytcher is he that will drinke out his thrift at the ale or wine, and be oft times dronke. This is a licoryce knaue that will swill his Maisters drink, and brybe his meate that is kept for him.

8 JEFFREY GODS FO.

Jeffery Gods Fo is he, that wil sweare & maintaine [leaf 8] othes. This is such a lying knaue that none wil beleue him, for the more he sweareth, ye les he is to be beleued.

9 NICHOL HARTLES.

Nichol Hartles is he, that when he should do ought for his Maister hys hart faileth him. This is a Trewand knaue that faineth himselfe sicke when he should woorke.

10 SIMON SOONE AGON.

Simon soone agon is he, that when his Mayster hath any thing to do, he wil hide him out of the way. This is a loytring knaue that wil hide him in a corner and sleepe or els run away.

11 GRENE WINCHARD.

Greene Winchard is he, that when his hose is broken and hange out at his shoes, he will put them into his shooes againe with a stick, but he wyll not amend them. This is a slouthfull knaue, that had leauer go lyke a begger then cleanly.

12 PROCTOUR.

Proctour is he, that will tary long, and bring a lye, when his Maister sendeth him on his errand. This is a stibber gibber Knaue, that doth fayne tales.

13 COMMITOUR OF TIDINGES.

Commitour of Tidings is he, that is ready to bring his Maister Nouels and tidinges, whether they be true or false. This is a tale bearer knaue, that wyll report words spoken in his Maisters presence.

14 GYLE HATHER

Gyle Hather is he, that wyll stand by his Maister when he is at dinner, and byd him beware that he eate no raw meate, because he would eate it himselfe. This is a pickthanke knaue, that would make his Maister [leaf 8 b.] beleue that the Cowe is woode.

15 BAWDE PHISICKE.

Bawde Phisicke, is he that is a Cocke, when his Maysters meate is euyll dressed, and he challenging him therefore, he wyl say he wyll eate the rawest morsel thereof him selfe. This is a sausye knaue, that wyl contrary his Mayster alway.

16 MOUNCH PRESENT.

Mounch present is he that is a great gentleman, for when his Mayster sendeth him with a present, he wil take a tast thereof by the waye. This is a bold knaue, that sometyme will eate the best and leaue the worst for his Mayster.

17 COLE PROPHET.

Cole Prophet is he, that when his Maister sendeth him on his errand, he wyl tel his answer therof to his Maister or he depart from hym. This tittiuell knaue commonly maketh the worst of the best betwene hys Maister and his friende.

18 CORY FAUELL.

Cory fauell is he, that wyl lye in his bed, and cory the bed bordes in which hee lyeth in steede of his horse. This slouthfull knaue wyll buskill and scratch when he is called in the morning, for any hast.

19 DYNG THRIFT.

Dyng thrift is he, that wil make his Maisters horse eate pies and rybs of beefe, and drinke ale and wyne. Such false knaues oft tymes, wil sell their Maisters meate to their owne profit.

20 ESEN DROPPERS.

Esen Droppers bene they, that stand vnder mens wales or windowes, or in any other place, to heare the [leaf 9] secretes of a mans house. These misdeming knaues wyl stand in corners to heare if they be euill spoken of, or waite a shrewd turne.

21 CHOPLOGYKE.

Choplogyke, is he that when his mayster rebuketh him of hys fault he wyll geue hym .xx. wordes for one, els byd the deuils Pater noster in silence. This proude prating knaue wyll maintaine his naughtines when he is rebuked for them.

22 VNTHRIFTE.

Vnthrift, is he that wil not put his wearing clothes to washing, nor black his owne shoes, nor amend his his (*sic*) own wearing clothes. This rechles knaue wyl alway be lousy: and say that hee hath no more shift of clothes, and slaunder his Maister.

23 VNGRACIOUS.

Vngracious, is he *that* by his own will, will heare no maner of seruice, without he be compelled therunto by his rulers. This Knaue wil sit at the alehouse drinking or playing at dice, or at other games at seruice tyme.

24 NUNQUAM.

Nunquam, is he that when his Maister sendeth him on his errand he wil not come againe of an hour or two where he might haue done it in halfe an houre or lesse. This knaue will go about his owne errand or pastime and saith he cannot speede at the first.

25 INGRATUS.

Ingratus, is he that when one doth all that he can for him, he will scant geue him a good report for his labour. This knaue is so ingrate or vnkind, *th*at he considreth not his frend from his fo, & wil requit euil for good & being put most in trust, wil sonest deceiue his maister.

FINIS.

[leaf 9 b.] Imprinted at London by
Iohn Awdely dwelling
in little Britaine streete
without Aldersgate.

(. •.)

[Original in Bodleian Library, 4°. R. 21. Art. Seld.]

A Caueat or Warening,

FOR COMMEN CVRSE-

TORS VVLGARELY CALLED

Vagabones, set forth by Thomas Harman,

Esquiere, for the vtilite and proffyt of his naturall

Cuntrey. Augmented and inlarged by the fyrst author here of.

Anno Domini. M.D.LXVII.

¶ *Vewed, examined, and allowed, according vnto the Queenes Maiestyes Iniunctions.*

¶ Imprinted at London, in Fletestrete, at the signe of the Falcon, by *Wylliam Gryffith*, and are to be sold at his shoppe in Saynt Dunstones Churche yarde, in the West.
Anno Domini. 1567.

[The Bodley edition of 1567 omits 'or Warening' in line 1, and 'Anno Domini. 1567.' at foot; and substitutes 'Newly Augmented and Imprinted' for 'Augmented ... here of', line 6.]

[leaf 2]

¶ To the ryght honorable and my singular good Lady, Elizabeth Countes of Shrewsbury, Thomas Harman wisheth all ioye and perfite felicitie, here and in the worlde to come.

AS of Auncient and longe tyme there hath bene, and is now at this present, many good, godly, profitable lawes and actes made and setforthe in this most noble and floryshynge realme, for the reliefe, succour, comforte, and sustentacion of the poore, nedy, impotent, and myserable creatures beinge and inhabiting in all parts of the same; So is there (ryghte honorable and myne especyall good Lady) most holsom estatutes, ordinances, and necessary lawes, made, setforth, and publisshed, for the extreme punishement of all vagarantes and sturdy vacabons, as passeth throughe and by all parts of this famous yle, most idelly and wyckedly: and I wel, by good experience, vnderstandinge and consideringe your most tender, pytyfull, gentle, and noble nature,—not onelye hauinge a vygelant and mercifull eye to your poore, indygente, and feable parishnores; yea, not onely in the parishe where your honour moste happely doth dwell, but also in others inuyroninge or nighe adioyning to the same; As also aboundantly powringe out dayely your ardent and bountifull charytie vppon all such as commeth for reliefe vnto your luckly gates,—

I thought it good, necessary, and my bounden dutye, to acquaynte your goodnes with the abhominable, wycked, and detestable behauor of all these rowsey, ragged rabblement of rakehelles, that—vnder the pretence of great misery, dyseases, and other innumerable calamites whiche they fayne—through great hipocrisie do wyn and gayne great almes in all places where they wyly wander, to the vtter deludinge of the good geuers, deceauinge and impouerishing of all such poore housholders, both sicke and sore, as nether can or maye walke abroad for reliefe and comforte (where, in dede, most mercy is to be shewed). And for that I (most honorable Lady), beinge placed as a poore gentleman, haue kepte a house these twenty yeares, where vnto pouerty dayely hath and doth repayre, not without some reliefe, as my poore callinge and habylytie maye and doth extende : I haue of late yeares gathered a great suspition that all should not be well, and, as the prouerbe saythe, "sume thinge lurke and laye hyd that dyd not playnely apeare;" for I, hauinge more occation, throughe sickenes, to tary and remayne at home then I haue bene acustomed, do, by my there abyding, talke [1] and confere dayly with many of these wyly wanderars of both sortes, as well men and wemmen, as boyes and gyrles, by whom I haue [leaf 2, back] gathered and vnderstande their depe dissimulation and detestable dealynge, beinge maruelous suttle and craftye in there kynde, for not one amongst twenty wyll discouer, eyther declare there scelorous secretes : yet with fayre flatteringe wordes, money, and good chere, I haue attained to the typ by such as the meanest of them hath wandred these xiii. yeares, and most xvi. and some twenty and vpward,[2] and not withoute faythfull promesse made vnto them neuer to discouer their names or any thinge they shewed me ; for they would all saye, yf the vpright men should vnderstand thereof, they should not be only greuouslye beaten, but put in daunger of their lyues, by the sayd vpright men. There was a fewe yeares since a small bréefe setforth of some zelous man to his countrey, of whom I knowe not, that made a lytle shewe of there names and vsage, and gaue a glymsinge lyghte, not sufficient to perswade of their peuishe peltinge and pickinge [3] practyses, but well worthy of prayse. But (good madame), with nolesse trauell then good wyll, I haue repayred and rygged the Shyp of knowledge, and haue hoyssed vp the sayles of good fortune, that

---

[1] leaf 2 b. Bodley edition (B).
[2] The severe Act against vagrants, Ed. VI., c. 3, was passed in 1548, only 19 years before the date of this 2nd edition.
[3] The 1573 edition reads *pynking*

she maye safely passe aboute and through all partes of this noble realme, and there make porte sale of her wyshed wares, to the confusion of their drowsey demener and vnlawfull language, pylfring pycking, wily wanderinge, and lykinge lechery, of all these rablement of rascales that raunges about al t*h*e costes of the same, So *that* their vndecent, dolefull dealing and execrable exercyses. may apere to all as it were in a glasse, that therby the Iusticers *and* Shréeues may in their circutes be more vygelant to punishe these malefactores, and the Counstables, Bayliffes, and bosholders,[1] settinge asyde all feare, slouth, *and* pytie, may be more circomspect in executing the charg geuen them by the aforesayd Iusticers. Then wyll no more this rascall rablement raunge about the countrey. Then greater reliefe may be shewed to t*h*e pouerty of eche parishe. Then shall we kepe our Horses in our pastures vnstolen. Then our lynnen clothes shall and maye lye safelye one our hedges vntouched. Then shall we not haue our clothes and lynnen hoked out at our wyndowes as well by day as by night. Then shall we not haue our houses broken vp in the night, as of late one of my nyghtbors had and two great buckes of clothes stolen out, and most of the same fyne Lynnen. Then shall we safely kepe our pigges and poultrey from pylfring. Then shall we surely passe by [2]t*h*e hygh waies leading to markets *and* fayres vnharmed. Then shall our Shopes and bothes be vnpycked *and* spoyled. Then shall these vncomly companies be dispersed and set to labour for their lyuinge, or hastely hang for [leaf 3] their demerites. Then shall it incourrage a great number of gentle men and others, seing this securitie, to set vp houses and kepe hospitalytie in the countrey, to the comfort of their nighboures, releife of the poore, and to the amendement of the common welth. Then shall not sinne and wickednes so much abound among vs. Then wil gods wrath be much t*h*e more pacified towards vs. Then shall we not tast of so many and sondry plages, as now dayely raigneth ouer vs. And then shall this Famous Empyre be in more welth *and* better florysh, to the inestymable ioye *and* comfort of the Quenes most excelent maiestye, whom god of his

---

[1] So printed in both 1567 editions. 1573 reads *housholders ;* but *Borsholders* is doubtless meant.   [2] leaf 3. B.

infinyte goodnes, to his great glory, long and many yeares make most prosperously to raygne ouer vs, to the great Felycitye of all the Peres and Nobles, and to the vnspeakable ioye, releife, and quietnes of minde, of all her faythfull Commons *and* Subiectes. Now, me thinketh, I se how these peuysh, peruerse, and pestilent people begyn to freat, fume, sweare, and stare at this my booke, their lyfe being layd open and aparantly paynted out, that their confusion and end draweth one a pase. Where as in dede, if it be well waied, it is set forth for their synguler profyt and commoditie, for the sure safegard of their lyues here in this world, that they shorten not the same before [1] their time, and that by their true labour and good lyfe, in the world to com they may saue their Soules, that Christ, the second person in [the] Trinytie, hath so derely bought wit*h* his most precious bloud : so that hereby I shall do them more good then they could haue deuised for them selues. For behold, their lyfe being so manyfest wycked and so aparantlye knowen, The honorable wyl abhore them, The worshipfull wyll reiecte them, The yemen wyll sharpely tawnte them, The Husband men vtterly defye them, The laboryng men bluntly chyde them, The wemen with a loud exclamation [2] wonder at them, And all Children with clappinge handes crye out at them. I manye times musing with my selfe at these mischeuous misliuers, merueled when they toke their oryginall *and* beginning ; how long they haue exercised their execrable wandring about. I thought it méete to confer with a very old man that I was well acquaynted with, whose wyt *and* memory is meruelous for his yeares, beinge about the age of fourescore, what he knewe when he was yonge of these lousey leuterars. And he shewed me, that when he was yonge he wayted vpon a man of much worshyp in Kent, who died immediatly after the last Duke of Buckingham was beheaded : at his buryall there was such a number of beggers, besides poore housholders dwelling there abouts, that vnneth they mighte lye or stande aboute the House: then was there [leaf 3, back] prepared for them a great and a large barne, and a great fat oxe sod out in Furmenty for them, with bread *and* drinke aboundantly to furnesh out the premisses ; and euery person had two pence, for such was the

[1] Printed "*brfore*"   [2] *reclamation*. B.

dole. When Night approched, *the* pore housholders repaired home to their houses: the other wayfaring bold beggers remained alnight in *the* barne; and the same barne being serched with light in the night by this old man (and then yonge), with [1] others, they tolde seuen score persons of men, euery of them hauing his woma*n*, except it were two wemen that lay alone to gether for some especyall cause. Thus hauing their makes to make mery withall, the buriall was turned to bousing *and* belly chere, morning to myrth, fasting to feasting, prayer to pastyme *and* pressing of papes, and lamenting to Lechery. So that it may apere this vncomly company hath had a long continuance, but then nothinge geuen so much to pylferinge, pyckinge, and spoyling; and, as far as I can learne or vnderstand by the examination of a number of them, their languag—which they terme peddelars Frenche or Canting—began but within these xxx. yeeres,[2] lytle aboue; and that the first inuenter therof was hanged, all saue the head; for that is the fynall end of them all, or els to dye of some filthy and horyble diseases: but much harme is don in the meane space by their continuance, as some x., xii., and xvi. yeares before they be consumed, and the number of them doth dayly renew. I hope their synne is now at the hyghest; and that as short and as spedy a redresse wylbe for these, as hath bene of late yeres for *the* wretched, wily, wandering vagabonds calling and naming them selues Egiptians, depely dissembling and long hyding *and* couering their depe, decetfull practises,—feding the rude common people, wholy addicted and geuen to nouelties, toyes, and new inuentions,— delyting them with the strangenes of the attyre of their heades, and practising paulmistrie to such as would know their fortunes: And, to be short, all theues and hores (as I may well wryt),—as some haue had true experience, a number can well wytnes, and a great sorte hath well felte it. And now (thankes bée to god), throughe wholsome lawes, and the due execution thereof, all be dispersed, banished,[3] *and* the memory of them cleane extynguished; that when they bée once named here after, our Chyldren wyll muche meruell what kynd of people they were: and so, I trust, shal shortly happen of these.

[1] The 1573 edition reads *and*
[2] The 1573 edition here inserts the word *or*
[3] *vanished.* B.

For what thinge doth chiefely cause these rowsey rakehelles thus to continue and dayly increase? Surely a number of wicked parsons that kéepe typlinge Houses in all shires, where they haue succour and reliefe; and what so euer they bring, they are sure to receaue money for [leaf 4] the same, for they sell good penyworthes. The byers haue *th*e greatest gayne; yea, yf they haue nether money nor ware, they wylbe trusted; their credite is much. I haue taken a note of a good many of them, *and* wil send their names and dwelling-places to such Iusticers as dwelleth nere or next vnto them, that they by their good wisdomes may displace the same, and auctoryse such as haue honesty. I wyl not blot my boke with their names, because they be resident. But as for this fletinge Fellowshyp, I haue truly setforth the most part of them that be doers at this present, with their names that they be knowene by. Also, I haue placed in the end therof their leud language, calling the same pedlers French or Canting. And now shal I end my prologue, makinge true declaration (right honorable Lady) as they shal fall in order of their vntymelye tryfelinge time, leud lyfe, and pernitious practises, trusting that the same shall neyther trouble or abash your most tender, tymerous, and pytifull Nature, to thinke the smal mede should growe vnto you for such Almes so geuen. For god, our marcifull and most louing father, well knoweth your hartes and good intent,—the geuer neuer wanteth his reward, according to the sayinge of Saynt Augustyn: as there is (neyther shalbe) any synne vnpunished, euen so shall there not be eny good dede vnrewarded. But how comfortably speaketh Christ our Sauiour vnto vs in his gospel ("geue ye, and it shalbe geuen you againe"): behold farther, good Madam, that for a cup of colde water, Christ hath promised a good reward. Now saynt Austen properly declareth why Christ speaketh of colde water, because the poorest man that is shall not excuse him selfe from that cherytable warke, least he would, parauenture, saye that he hath neyther wood, pot, nor pan to warme any water with. Se, farther, what god speaketh in the mouth of his prophet, Esaye, "breake thy bread to him that is a hongred;" he sayth not geue him a hole lofe, for paraduenture the poore man hath it not to geue, then let him geue a pece. This much is sayd because the poore that hath it should not

be excused : now how much more then the riche? Thus you se, good
madam, for your treasure here dispersed, where nede and lacke
is, it shalbe heaped vp aboundantly for you in heauen,
where neither rust or moth shall corupt or destroy
the same. Vnto which tryumphant place, after
many good, happy, and fortunat yeres pros-
perouslye here dispended. you maye for
euer and euer there most ioyfully
remayne. A men.

¶¶ *FINIS*

Thre things to be noted   all in their kynde
A staff, a béesom, and   wyth, that wyll wynde

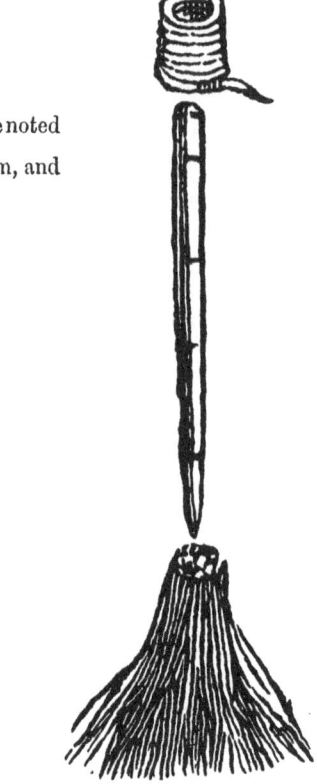

¶ A béesome of byrche, for babes very feete,[1]
   A longe lastinge lybbet for loubbers as méete
   A wyth to wynde vp, that these wyll not kéepe
   Bynde all up in one, and vse it to swéepe

[This page is printed at the back of the title page in Bodley edition.]
[1] *fyt*. B.

¶ THE EPISTLE TO THE READER. [leaf 5]

AL though, good Reader, I wright in plain termes—and not so playnly as truely—concerning the matter, meaning honestly to all men, and wyshe them as much good as to myne owne harte; yet, as there hathe bene, so there is nowe, and hereafter wylbe, curyous heds to finde fauttes: wherefore I thought it necessary, now at this seconde Impression, to acquaynt the with a great faulte, as some takethe it, but none[1] as I meane it, callinge these Vagabonds Cursetors in the intytelynge of my booke, as runneres or rangers aboute the countrey, deriued of this Laten word (*Curro*): neither do I wryght it Cooresetores, with a duble[2] oo; or Cowresetors, with a w, which hath an other singnification: is there no deuersite betwen a gardein and a garden, maynteynaunce *and* maintenance, Streytes and stretes? those that haue vnderstanding knowe there is a great dyfference: who is so ignorant by these dayes as knoweth not the meaning of a vagabone? and yf an ydell leuterar should be so called of eny man, would not he think it botne odyous and reprochefull? wyll he not shonne the name? ye, and where as he maye and dare, with bent browes, wyll reueng that name of Ingnomy: yet this playne name vagabone is deryued, as others be, of Laten wordes, and now vse makes it commen to al men; but let vs loke back four .C. yeres sithens, *and* let vs se whether this playn word vagabon was vsed or no. I beleue not, and why? because I rede of no such name in the old estatutes of this realme, vnles it be in the margente of the booke, or in the Table, which in the collection and pryntinge was set in; but these were then the commen names of these leud leuterars, Faytores, Robardesmen, Drawlatches, *and* valyant beggares. Yf I should haue vsed suche wordes, or the same order of wryting, as this realme vsed in Kynge Henry the thyrd or Edward the fyrstes tyme, oh, what a grose, barberous fellow [leaf 5, back] haue we here! his wryting is both homely and darke, that wee had nede to haue an interpretar: yet then it was verye well, and in short season a great change we see. well, this delycat age shall haue his tyme on the

---

[1] The 1573 ed. reads *not*.
[2] This word is omitted in the 1573 ed.

other syde. Eloquence haue I none; I neuer was acquaynted with the muses; I neuer tasted of Helycon. But accordinge to my playne order, I haue setforth this worke, symplye and truelye, with such vsual words and termes as is among vs wel known and frequented. So that as *th*e prouerbe saythe, "all though truth be blamed, it shal neuer be shamed." well, good reader, I meane not to be tedyous vnto the, but haue added fyue or sixe more tales, because some of them weare donn whyle my booke was fyrste in the presse; and as I truste I haue deserued no rebuke for my good wyll, euen so I desyre no prayse for my payne, cost, and trauell. But faithfullye for the proffyt and benyfyt of my countrey I haue don it, that the whole body of the Realme may se and vnderstand their lewd lyfe and pernitious practisses, that all maye spedelye helpe to amend that is amysse. Amen saye all with me.

Finis

¶ A RUFFLER. Ca. 1.[1] [leaf 6]

THE Rufflar, because he is first in degre of this odious order: And is so called in a statute made for the punishment of Vacabonds, In the xxvij. yeare of Kyng Henry the eight, late of most famous memory: Hée shall be first placed, as the worthiest of this vnruly rablement. And he is so called when he goeth first abroad; eyther he hath serued in the warres, or els he hath bene a seruinge man; and, weary of well doing, shakinge of all payne, doth chuse him this ydle lyfe, and wretchedly wanders aboute the most shyres of this realme. And with stout audacyte, [2] demaundeth where he thinketh hée maye be bolde, and circomspecte ynough, as he sethe cause to aske charitie, rufully and lamentably, that it would make a flyntey hart to relent, and pytie his miserable estate, howe he hath bene maymed and broused in the warres; *and*, parauenture, some wyll shew you some outward wounde, whiche he gotte at some dronken fraye, eyther haltinge of some preuye wounde festred with a fylthy firy flankard. For be well assured that the hardist souldiers be eyther slayne or maymed, eyther and[3] they escape all hassardes, and retourne home agayne, if they bée without reliefe of their friends, they wyl surely desperatly robbe and steale, and [4] eyther shortlye be hanged or miserably dye in pryson; for they be so much ashamed and disdayne to beg or aske charity, that rather they wyll as desperatlye fight for to lyue and mayntayne them selues, as manfully and valyantly they ventred them selues in the Prynces quarell. Now these Rufflars, the out castes of seruing men, when begginge or crauinge fayles, then they pycke and pylfer, from other inferiour beggeres that they méete by the waye, as Roages, Pallyardes, Mortes, and Doxes. Yea, if they méete with a woman alone ridinge to the market, eyther olde man or boye, that hée well knoweth wyll not resiste, such they filche and spoyle. These rufflars, after a yeare or two at the farthest, become vpryght men, vnlesse they be preuented by twind hempe.

---

[1] The chapters are not noted in the Bodley ed.
[2] The 1573 ed. here inserts the word *he*
[3] 1573 reads *if*   [4] 1573 has *or*

{ I had of late yeares an old man to my tennant, who customably a greate tyme went twise in the wéeke to London, eyther wyth fruite or with pescodes, when tyme serued therefore. And as he was comminge homewarde on blacke heathe, at the end thereof next to shotars hyl, he ouer tooke two rufflars, the one manerly wayting on the other, as one had ben the maister, *and* the other the man or seruant, [leaf 6, back] caryinge his maisteres cloke. this olde man was verye glad that hee might haue their company ouer the hyl, because that day he had made a good market; for hée had seuen shyllinges in his purse, and a nolde angell, which this poore man had thought had not bene in his purse, for hée wylled his wyfe ouer night to take out the same angell, and laye it vp vntyll his comminge home agayne. And he verely thought that his wyfe had so don, whiche in dede for got to do it. Thus after salutations had, this maister rufflar entered into communication with this simple olde man, who, ridinge softlye beside them, commoned of many matters. Thus fedinge this old man with pleasaunt talke, vntyll they weare one the toppe of the hyll, where these rufflares might well beholde the coaste about them cleare, Quiclye stepes vnto this poore man, and taketh holde of his horse brydell, and leadeth him in to the wode, and demaundeth of him what and how much money he had in his purse. "Now, by my troth," quoth this old man; "you are a merrye gentle man. I knowe you meane not to take a waye anye thinge from me, but rather to geue me some if I shoulde aske it of you." By and by, this seruant thiefe casteth the cloke that he caried on his arme about this poore mans face, that he should not marke or vew them, with sharpe words to delyuer quicly that he had, and to confesse truly what was in his purse. This poore man, then all abashed, yelded, and confessed that he had but iust seuen shyllinges in his purse; and the trouth is he knew of no more. This old angell was falen out of a lytle purse into the botome of a great purse. Now, this seuen shyllings in whyte money they quickly founde, thinkinge in dede that there had bene no more; yet farther groping and searchinge, found this old angell. And with great admiraticn, this gentleman thyefe begane to blesse hym, sayinge, "good lorde, what a worlde is this! howe maye" (quoth hée) "a man beleue or truste in the same? se you not" (quoth he) "this old knaue tolde me that he had but seuen shyllings, and here is more by an angell: what an old knaue and a false knaue haue we here!" quoth this rufflar; "oure lorde haue mercy on vs, wyll this worlde neuer be better?"—and there with went their waye. And lefte the olde man in the wood, doinge him no more harme. But sorowfully sighinge, this olde man, returning home, declared his misaduenture, with all the words and circumstaunces aboue shewed. Wherat, for the tyme was great laughing, and this poore man for his losses among his louing neighboures well considered in the end.

¶ A VPRIGHT MAN. Ca. 2.

[leaf 7] A Vpright[1] man, the second in secte of this vnsemely sorte, must be next placed, of these rainginge rablement of rascales; some be seruing men, artificers, and laboryng men traded vp in husbandry. These not mindinge to get their lyuinge with the swete of their face, but casting of all payne, wyll wander, after their wycked maner, through the most shyres of this realm,—

As Sommerset shyre, Wylshire, Barke shyre, Oxforde shyre, Harfordeshyre, Myddilsex, Essex, Suffolke, Northfolke, Sussex, Surrye, and Kent, as the cheyfe and best shyres of reliefe. Yea, not with out punishment by stockes, whyppinges, and imprisonment, in most of these places aboue sayde. Yet, not with standinge they haue so good lykinge in their lewed, lecherous loyteringe, that full quiclye all their punishmentes is[2] for gotten. And repentaunce is neuer thought vpon vntyll they clyme thrée tres with a ladder. These vnrewly rascales, in their roylynge, disperse them selues into seuerall companyes, as occation serueth, sometyme more and somtyme lesse. As, if they repayre to a poore husbandmans house, hée wyll go a lone, or one with him, and stoutely demaund his charytie, eyther shewing how he hath serued in the warres, and their maymed, eyther that he sekethe seruice, and saythe that he woulde be glad to take payne for hys lyuinge, althoughe he meaneth nothinge lesse.

[1] Printed "*vpreght.*" *vpright* in Bodley ed.
[2] 1573, *be*

Yf he be offered any meate or drynke, he vtterlye refusethe scornefully, and wyll nought but money; and yf he espye yong pyges or pultry, he well noteth the place, and they the next night, or shortly after, hée wyll be sure to haue some of them, whyche they brynge to their stawlinge kens, which is their typplyng houses, as well knowen to them, according to the olde prouerbe, "as the begger knowes his dishe." For you must vnderstand, euery Typplyng ale house wyll neyther receiue them or their wares, but some certayne houses in euery shyre, especially for that purpose, where they shalbe better welcome to them then honester men. For by such haue they most gayne, and shalbe conuayde eyther into some loft out of the waye, or other secret corner not commen to any other; and thether repayre, at accustomed tymes, their harlots, whiche they terme Mortes and Doxes,—not with emty hands; for they be as skilfull in picking, riffling, *and* filching as the vpright men, and nothing inferior to them in all kind of wyckednes, as in other places hereafter they shalbe touched. At these foresayde peltinge, peuish places and vnmannerly metinges, O! how the pottes walke about! their talki*n*g tounges talke at large. They bowle and bowse one to another, and for the tyme bousing belly chere. And after there ruysting recreation, [leaf 7, back] yf there be not rome ynough in the house, they haue cleane strawe in some barne or backehouse nere adioyning, where they couch comly to gether, and [1] it were dogge and byche; and he that is hardyste maye haue his choyse, vnlesse for a lytle good maner; some wyll take there owne that they haue made promyse vnto, vntyll they be out of sight, and then, according to the old adage, "out of minde." Yet these vpright men stand so much vpon their reputation, as they wyl in no case haue their wemen walke with them, but seperat them selues for a tyme, a moneth or more. And mete at fayres, or great markets, where they mete to pylfer and steale from staules, shoppes, or bothes. At these fayres the vpryght men vse commonly to lye *and* lingar in hye wayes by lanes, some prety way or distaunce from *th*e place, by which wayes they be assured that compeny passeth styll two and fro. And ther they [2] wyll demaund, with cap in hand and comly curtesy, the deuotion and charity of *th*e people. They

[1] 1573, *as* [2] *the*. B.

haue ben much lately whipped at fayrs. Yf they aske at a stout yemans or farmars house his charity, they wyll goe strong as thre or foure in a company. Where for feare more then good wyll, they often haue reliefe. they syldome or neuer passe by a Iustices house, but haue by wayes, vnlesse he dwell alone, and but weakely manned; thether wyll they also go strong, after a slye, suttle sorte, as with their armes bounde vp with kercher or lyste, hauinge wrapte about the same filthy clothes, either their legges in such maner bewrapped halting down right. Not vnprouided of good codg[e]ls, which they cary to sustayne them, and, as they fayne, to kéepe gogges[1] from them, when they come to such good gentlemens houses. Yf any searche be made or they suspected for pylfring clothes of hedgges, or breaking of houses, which they commonly do when the owners bée eyther at the market, church, or other wayes occupied aboute their busines,—eyther robbe some sely man or woman by the hye waye, as many tymes they do,—Then they hygh them into wodes, great thickets, and other ruffe corners, where they lye lurkinge thre or foure dayes to gether, and haue meate and drinke brought them by theyre Mortes, and Doxes; and whyle they thus lye hydden in couert, in the night they be not idle,—nether, as t*h*e common saying is, " well occupyed;" for then, as the wyly foxe, crepinge out of his den, seketh his praye for pultery, so do these for lynnen and any thinge els worth money, that lyeth about or near a house. As somtyme a whole bucke of clothes caryed awaye at a tyme. When they haue a greatter booty then they maye cary awaye quickly to their stawling kendes, as is aboue sayd, They wyll hyde the same for a thre dayes in some thicke couert, and [leaf 8] in the night time carye the same, lyke good water Spanlles, to their foresayd houses. To whom they wyll discouer where or in what places they had the same, where the markes shalbe pycked out cleane, *and* conuayed craftely fare of, to sell. If the man or woman of the house want money the*m* selues. [2] If these vpright men haue nether money nor wares, at these houses they shalbe trusted for their vitales, and it amount to twentye or thirty shyllings. Yea, if it fortune any of these vpright men to be taken, either suspected, or charged with fellony or petye

[1] *dogges.* B.   1573 inserts *and*

brybrye, don at such a tyme or such a place, he wyll saye he was in his hostes house. And if the man or wyfe of that house be examined by an officer, they boldelye vouche, that the[y] lodged him suche a tyme, whereby the truth cannot appeare. And if they chaunce to be retained into seruice, through their lamentable words, with any welthy man, They wyll tary but a smale tyme, either robbing his maister or som of his fellowes. And some of them vseth this policye, that although they trauayle into al these shyres, aboue said, yet wyl they haue good credite, espiciallye in one shyre, where at diuers good farmars houses they be wel knowen, where they worke a moneth in a place or more, and wyll for that time behaue them selues very honestly *and* paynfully ; And maye at any tyme, for their good vsage, haue worke of them ; and to these at a ded lyft, or last refuge, they maye safely repayre vnto and be welcom, When in other places, for a knacke of knauery that they haue playd, thei dare not tary. These vyright men wil sildom or neuer want ; for what is gotten by anye Mort, or Doxe, if it please him, hée doth comaunde the same. And if he mete any begger, whether he be sturdye or impotent, he wyll demaund of him, whether euer he was stalled to the roge or no. If he saye he was, he wyll know of whom, and his name *tha*t stalled hym. And if he be not learnedly able to shewe him the whole circumstaunce thereof, he wyll spoyle him of his money, either of his best garment, if it be worth any money, and haue him to the bowsing ken, Which is to some typpling house next adioyninge ; and laieth their to gage the best thing that he hath for twenty pence or two shyllinges : this man obeyeth for feare of beating. Then doth this vpright man call for a gage of bowse, whiche is a quarte pot of drinke, and powres the same vpon his peld pate, adding these words :—" I. G. P. do stalle thée W. T. to the Roge, and that from hence forth it shall be lawefull for the to Cant "—that is, to aske or begge—" for thy liuing in al places." Here you se *tha*t the vpright man is of great auctorite. For all sortes of beggers are obedient to his hests, and surmounteth all others in pylfring and stealinge. ¶ I lately had standinge in my [leaf 8, back] well house, which standeth on the backeside of my house, a great cawdron of copper, beinge then full of water, hauinge in the same halfe a doson of pewter dyshes, well marked, and stamped with the connizance of my armes, whiche being well noted when they were taken out, were set a side, the water powred out, and my caudren taken awaye, being of such bygnes that one man, vnlesse he were of great strength, was not able far to cary the same. Not withstandinge, the same was one night within this two yeares conuayed more then half a myle from my house, into a commen or heth, And ther bestowed in a great firbushe. I then immediatly the next day sent one of my men to London, and there gaue warning in Sothwarke, kent strete, and Barmesey stréete, to all the Tynckars there dwelling,—That if any such Caudron came thether to be sold, the bringar therof should be stayed, and promised twenty shyllings for a reward. I gaue also intelligence to the water men that kept the ferres, that no such vessel should be ether conuayd to London or into essex, promysing the lyke reward, to haue vnderstanding therof. This my doing was well vnderstand in many places about, and that the feare of espyinge so troubled the conscience of the stealer, that my caudoren laye vntouched in the thicke firbushe more then halfe a yeare after, which, by a great chaunce, was found by hunteres for conneys; for one chaunced to runne into the same bushe where my caudren was, and being perceaued, one thrust his staffe into the same bushe, and hyt my caudren a great blowe, the sound whereof dyd cause the man to thinke and hope that there was some great treasure hidden, wherby he thought to be the better whyle he lyued. And in farther searching he found my caudren; so had I the same agayne vnloked for.

¶ A HOKER, OR ANGGLEAR. Cap. 3.

These hokers, or Angglers, be peryllous and most wicked knaues, and be deryued or procede forth from the vpright men; they commenly go in frese ierkynes and gally slopes, poynted benethe the kne; these when they practise there pylfringe, it is all by night; for, as they walke a day times from house to house, to demaund charite, they vigelantly marke where or in what place they maye attayne to there praye, casting there eyes vp to euery wyndow, well noting what they se their, whether apparell or linnen, hanginge nere vnto the sayde wyndowes, and that wyll they be sure to haue t*h*e next night folowing ; for they customably carry with them a staffe of v. or vi. foote long, in which, within one ynch of t*h*e tope therof, ys a lytle hole bored through, [leaf 9] in which hole they putte an yron hoke, and with the same they wyll pluck vnto them quickly any thing *that* they may reche ther with, which hoke in the day tyme they couertly cary about them, and is neuer sene or taken out till they come to the place where they worke there fete : such haue I sene at my house, and haue oft talked with them and haue handled ther staues, not then vnderstanding to what vse or inte*n*t they serued, although I hadde and perceiued, by there talke and behauiour, great lykelyhode of euyll suspition in them : they wyl ether leane vppon there staffe, to hyde the hole thereof, when they talke with you, or holde their hande vpon the hole ; and what stuffe, either wollen or lynnen, they thus hoke out, they neuer carye the same forth with to their staulyng kens, but hides the same a iij. daies in some secret corner, *and* after conuayes the same to their houses abouesaid, where their host or hostys geueth them money for the same, but halfe the value that it is worth, or els their doxes shall a farre of sell the same at the like houses. I was credebly informed that a hoker came to a farmers house in the ded of the night, and putting back a drawe window of a low chamber, the bed standing hard by the sayd wyndow, in which laye three parsones (a man and two bygge boyes), this hoker with his staffe plucked of their garme*n*ts which lay vpon them to kepe them warme, with the couerlet and shete, and lefte them lying a slepe naked sauing there shertes, and had a way all clene, and neuer could vnderstande where it became. I verely suppose that when they wer wel waked with cold, they suerly thought that Robin goodfelow (accordinge to the old saying) had bene with them that night.

¶ A ROGE. Cap. 4.

A Roge is neither so stoute or hardy as the vpright man. Many of them will go fayntly and looke piteously when they sée, either méete any person, hauing a kercher, as white as my shooes, tyed about their head, with a short staffe in their hand, haltinge, although they nede not, requiring almes of such as they méete, or to what house they shal com. But you may easely perceiue by their colour *that* thei cary both health and hipocrisie about them, wherby they get gaine, when others want that cannot fayne and dissemble. Others therebee that walke sturdely about *the* countrey, *and* faineth to seke a brother or kinsman of his, dwelling within som part of *the* shire ;—ether that he hath a letter to deliuer to som honest housholder, dwelling out of an other Shyre, and will shewe you the same fayre sealed, with the superscription to [leaf 9, back] the partye he speaketh of, because you shall not thinke him to runne idelly about the countrey ;—either haue they this shyfte, they wyll cary a cirtificate or pasport about them from som Iusticer of the peace, with his hand and seale vnto the same, howe hée hath bene whipped and punished for a vacabonde according to the lawes of this realme, and that he muste returne to .T., where he was borne or last dwelt, by a certayne daye lymited in the same, whiche shalbe a good longe daye. And all this fayned, bycause without feare they woulde wyckedly wander, and wyll renue the same where or when it pleasethe them ; for they haue of their affinity that can wryte and read. These also wyll picke and steale as the vpright men, and hath their women and metinges at places apoynted, and nothinge to them inferiour in all kynde of knauery. There bée of these Roges Curtales, wearinge shorte clokes, that wyll chaunge their aparell, as occation seruethe. And their end is eyther hanginge, whiche they call trininge in their language, or die miserably of the pockes.

¶ There was not long sithens two Roges that alwaies did associate them selues together, *and* would neuer seperat them selues, vnles it were for some especiall causes, for they were sworn brothers, *and* were both of one age, and much like of favour : these two, trauelinge into east kent, resorted vnto an ale house there,[1] being weried with traueling, saluting with short curtisey, when they came into the house, such as thei sawe sitting there, in whiche company was the parson of the parish ; and callinge for a pot of the best ale, sat downe at the tables ende : the lykor liked them so well, that they had pot vpon pot, and sometyme, for a lytle good maner, would drinke and offer the cup to such as they best fancied ; and to be short, they sat

[1] 1573 omits.

out al the company, for eche man departed home aboute their busines. When they had well refreshed them selues, then these rowsy roges requested the good man of the house wyth his wyfe to sit downe and drinke with them, of whome they inquired what priest the same was, and where he dwelt: then they fayninge that they had an vncle a priest, and that he should dwel in these partes, which by all presumptions it should be he, and that they came of purpose to speake with hym, but because they had not sene hym sithens they were sixe yeares olde, they durst not be bold to take acquayntance of him vntyl they were farther instructed of the truth, and began to inquier of his name, and how longe he had dwelt there, and how farre his house was of from *th*e place they were in: the good wyfe of the house, thynkinge them honest men without disceit, because they so farre enquyred of their kinseman, was but of a good zelous naturall intent, shewed them cherefully that hee [leaf 10] was an honest man *and* welbeloued in the parish, and of good welth, *and* had ben there resident xv. years at the least; "but," saith she, "are you both brothers?" "yea, surely," said they, "we haue bene both in one belly, *and* were twinnes." "Mercy, god!" q*uoth* this folish woman; "it may wel be, for ye be not much vnlike,"—and wente vnto her hall windowe, callinge these yong men vnto her, and loking out therat;[1] pointed with her fingar *and* shewed them the house standing alone, no house nere the same by almoste a quarter of a myle; "that," sayd[2] she, "is your vncles house." "Nay," saith one of them, "he is not onely my vncle, but also my godfather." "It may well be," q*uoth* she, "nature wyll bind him to be the better vnto you." "Well," q*uoth* they, "we be weary, and meane not to trouble our vncle to-night; but to-morowe, god willinge, we wyll sée him and do our duty: but, I pray you, doth our vncle occupy husbandry? what company hath he in his house." "Alas!" saith she, "but one old woman *and* a boy, he hath no occupying at al: tushe," q*uoth* this good wyfe, "you be mad men; go to him this night, for hée hath better lodging for you then I haue, *and* yet I speake folishly against my[3] own profit, for by your taring[4] here I should gaine *th*e more by you." "Now, by my troth," q*uoth* one of them, "we thanke

[1] 1573 omits.   [2] *saith*. B.   [3] 1573, *myne*   [4] *tarying*. B.

you, good hostes, for your holsome councell, and we meane to do as you wyll vs: we wyl pause a whyle, and by that tyme it wylbe almost night; *and* I praye you geue vs a reckeninge,"—so, manerly paying for that they toke, bad their hoste and hostes farewell with takinge leaue of the cup, marched merelye out of the dores towardes this parsones house, vewed the same well rounde about, and passed by two bowshotes of into a younge wodde, where they laye consultinge what they shoulde do vntyll midnight. Quoth one of them, of sharper wyt and subtyller then the other, to hys fellowe, "thou seest that this house is stone walled about, and that we cannot well breake in, in any parte thereof; thou seest also that the windowes be thicke of mullions, that ther is no kreping in betwene: wherefore we must of necessytie vse some policye when strength wil not serue. I haue a horse locke here about me," saith he; "and this I hope shall serue oure turne." So when it was aboute xii. of the clocke, they came to the house and lurked nere vnto his chamber wyndowe: the dog of the house barked a good, that with they[1] noise, this priest waketh out of his sleepe, and began to cough and hem: then one of these roges stepes forth nerer the window *and* maketh a ruful *and* pityful noise, requiring for Christ sake[2] some reliefe, that was both hongry and thirstye, and was like to ly with out the dores all nighte and starue for colde, vnles he were releued by him with some small pece of money. "Where dwellest thou?" quoth this parson. "Alas! sir," saithe this roge, "I haue smal [leaf 10, back] dwelling, and haue com out of my way; and I should now," saith he, "go to any towne nowe at this time of night, they woulde set me in the stockes and punishe me." "Well," quoth this pitifull parson, "away from my house, either lye in some of my out houses vntyll the morning, and holde, here is a couple of pence for thee." "A god rewarde you," quoth this roge; "and in heauen may you finde it." The parson openeth his wyndowe, and thrusteth out his arme to geue his almes to this Roge that came whining to receiue it, and quickly taketh holde of his hand, and calleth his fellowe to him, whiche was redye at hande with the horse locke, and clappeth the same about the wrest of his arme, that the mullions standing so close together for strength, that for his

[1] So printed. Bodley ed. has *the*   [2] *sakes*. B.

life he could not plucke in his arme againe, and made him beleue, vnles he would at the least geue them .iii. li., they woulde smite of his arme from the body. So that this poore parson, in feare to lose his hand, called vp his olde woman that lay in the loft ouer him, and wylled her to take out all the money he had, which was iiij. markes, which he saide was all the money in his house, for he had lent vi. li. to one of his neighbours not iiij daies before. "Wel," q*uoth* they, "master parson, if you haue no more, vpon this condicion we wil take of the locke, that you will drinke .xij. pence for our sakes to-morow at the alehouse wher we found you, and thank the good wife for the good chere she made vs." He promised faithfully that he would so do; so they toke of the locke, and went their way so farre ere it was daye, that the parson coulde neuer haue any vnderstanding more of them. Now this parson, sorowfully slumbering that night betwene feare and hope, thought it was but folly to make two sorrowes of one; he vsed contentacion for his remedy, not forgetting in the morning to performe his promise, but went betims to his neighbour that kept tiplinge, and asked angerly where the same two men were that dranke with her yester daye. "Which two men?" q*uoth* this good wife. "The straungers that came in when I was at your house wyth my neighbores yesterday." "What! your neuewes?" q*uoth* she. "My neuewes?" q*uoth* this parson; "I trowe thou art mad." "Nay, by god!" q*uoth* this good[1] wife, "as sober as you; for they tolde me faithfully that you were their vncle: but, in fayth, are you not so in dede? for, by my trouth, they are strau[n]gers to me. I neuer saw them before." "O, out vpon them!" q*uoth* the parson; "they be false theues, and this night thei compelled me to geue them al the money in my house." "Benedicite!" q*uoth* this good wife, "*and* haue they so in dede? as I shall aunswere before god, one of them told me besides that you were godfather to him, and that he trusted to haue your blessinge before he departed." "What! did he?" quoth this parson; "a halter blesse him for [leaf 11] me!" "Me thinketh, by the masse, by your countenance you loked so wildly when you came in," quoth this good wife, "that somthing was amis." "I vse not to gest,"

[1] Omitted in 1573.

quoth this parson, "when I speake so earnestly." "Why, all your sorrowes goe with it," quoth this good wife, "and sitte downe here, and I will fil a freshe pot of ale shall make you mery agayne." "Yea," saith this parson, "fill in, *and* geue me some meat; for they made me sweare and promise them faithfully that I shoulde drinke xii. pence with you this day." "What! dyd they?" quoth she; "now, by the mary masse, they be mery knaues. I warraunt you they meane to bye no land with your money; but how could they come into you in the night, your dores being shut fast? your house is very stronge." Then this prason[1] shewed her all the hole circumstance, how he gaue them his almes oute at the wyndowe, they[2] made such lamentable crye that it pytied him at the hart; for he sawe but one when he put oute his hand at the windowe. "Be ruled by me," quoth this good wyfe. "Wherin?" quoth this parson. "By my troth, neuer speake more of it: when they shal vnderstand of it in the parish, they wyll but laugh you to skorne." [3]"Why, then," quoth this parson, "the deuyll goe with it,"—and their an end.[3]

¶ A WYLDE ROGE. Cap. 5.

A Wilde Roge is he that is borne a Roge: he is a more subtil and more geuen by nature to all kinde of knauery then the other, as beastely begotten in barne or bushes, and from his infancye traded vp in trechery; yea, and before ripenes of yeares doth permyt, wallowinge in lewde lechery, but that is counted amongest them no sin. For this is their custome, that when they mete in barne at night, euery one getteth a make[4] to lye wythall, *and* their chaunce to be twentye in a companye, as their is sometyme more and sometyme lesse: for to one man that goeth abroad, there are at the least two women, which neuer make it straunge when they be called, although she neuer knewe him before. Then when the day doth appeare, he rouses him vp, and shakes his eares, and awaye wanderinge where he may getto oughte to the hurte of others. Yet before he skyppeth oute of hys couche and departeth from his darling, if he like her well, he will apoint her where to mete shortlye

---

[1] so printed.   [2] *the*. B.
[3-3] Why . . . . end. B. omits.   [4] 1573 reads *mate*

after, with a warninge to worke warely for some chetes, that their meting might be the merier.

¶ Not long sithens, a wild roge chaunced to mete a pore neighbour of mine, who for honesty *and* good natur surmounteth many. This poore man, riding homeward from London, where he had made his market, this [leaf 11, back] roge demaunded a peny for gods sake, to kepe him a true man. This simple man, beholding him wel, and sawe he was of taule personage with a good quarter staffe in his hand, it much pitied him, as he sayd, to se him want; for he was well able to serue his prince in the wars. Thus, being moued with pytie, and[1] loked in his pursse to finde out a penye; and in loking for the same, he plucked oute viii. shyllinges in whyte money, and raked therin to finde a single peny; and at the last findinge one, doth offer the same to this wylde roge: but he, seinge so much mony in this simple mans hand, being striken to the hart with a couetous desire, bid him forth wyth delyuer al that he had, or els he woulde with his staffe beat out his braynes. For it was not a penye would now quench his thirst, [2]seing so much as he dyd[2]: thus, swallowinge his spittell gredely downe, spoyled this poore man of al *th*e money that he had, and lept ouer the hedge into a thicke wode, and went his waye as merely as this good simple man came home sorowfully. I once rebuking a wyld roge because he went idelly about, he shewed me that he was a begger by enheritance—his Grandfather was a begger, his father was one, and he must nedes be one by good reason.

¶ A PRYGGER OF PRAUNCERS. Cap. 6.

A Prigger of Praunercs be horse stealers; for to prigge signifieth in their language to steale, *and* a Prauncer is a horse: so beinge put together, the matter is[3] playne. These go commonly in Ierkins of leatherr, or of white frese, *and* carry litle wands in their hands, and will walke through grounds and pastures, to search and se horses meete for their purpose. And if thei chaunce to be met and asked by the owners of the grounde what they make there, they fayne strayghte that they haue loste their waye, and de-

---

[1] omitted in 1573.
[2-2] seing . . . . dyd. B. omits.   [3] 1573, *was*

syre to be enstructed the beste waye to such a place. These will also repayre to gentlemens houses and aske their charitye, and wyll offer their seruice. And if you aske them what they can do, they wyll saye that they can kepe two or thre Geldinges, and waite vppon a Gentleman. These haue also their women, that walkinge from them in other places, marke where and what they sée abroade, and sheweth these Priggars therof when they meete, which is with in a wéeke or two. And loke, where they steale any thinge, they conuay *th*e same at the least thre score miles of or more.

¶ There was a Gentleman, a verye friende of myne, rydyng from London homewarde into Kente, hauinge with in thrée myles of his house busynesse, alyghted of his horse, and his man also, in a pretye [leaf 12] vyllage, where diueres houses were, and looked aboute hym where he myghte haue a conuenient person to walke his horse, because hee would speake w*i*t*h* a Farmer that dwelt on the backe side of the sayde village, lytle aboue a quarter of a myle from the place where he lighted, and had his man to waight vpon him, as it was mete for his callinge : espying a Pryggar there standing, thinking the same to dwell there, charging this prity prigginge person to walke his horse well, and that they might not stande styll for takyng of colde, and at his returne (which he saide should not be longe) he would geue hym a peny to drinke, and so wente aboute his busines. This peltynge Priggar, proude of his praye, walkethe his horse[1] vp and downe tyll he sawe the Gentleman out of sighte, and leapes him into the saddell, and awaye he goeth a mayne. This Gentleman returninge, and findinge not his horses, sent his man to the one end of the vyllage, and he went himselfe vnto the other ende, and enquired as he went for his horses that were walked, and began some what to suspecte, because neither he nor his man could se nor find him. Then this Gentleman deligentlye enquired of thre or foure towne dwellers there whether any such person, declaring his stature,[2] age, apparell, with so many linaments of his body as he could call to remembraunce. And, "vna voce," all sayde that no such man dwelt in their streate, neither in the parish, that they knewe of ; but some did wel remember that such a one they saw there lyrkinge and hug-

---

[1] *horses.* B.   [2] Printed *statute*

geringe two houres before the Gentleman came thether, and a
straunger to them. "I had thoughte," quoth this Gentleman, "he
had here dwelled,"—and marched home manerly in his botes: farre
from the place he dwelt not. I suppose at his comming home he
sente suche wayes as he suspected or thought méete to searche for
this Prigger, but hetherto he neuer harde any tydinges agayne of his
palfreys.—I had the best geldinge stolen oute of my pasture that I
had amongst others whyle this boke was first a printinge.

¶ A PALLYARD. Cap. 7.

These Palliardes be called also Clapperdogens: these go with patched clokes, *and* haue their Morts with them, which they cal wiues; and if he goe to one house, to aske his almes, his wife shall goe to a nother: for what they get (as bread, chéese, malte, and woll) they sell the same for redy money; for so they get more and if they went together. Although they be thus[1] deuided in the daie, yet they mete iompe at night. Yf they chaunce to come to some gentylmans house standinge [leaf 12, back] a lone, and be demaunded whether they be man and wyfe, *and* if he perceaue that any doubteth thereof, he sheweth them a Testimonial with the ministers name, and others of the same parishe (naminge a parishe in some shere fare distant from the place where he sheweth the same). This writing he carieth to salue that sore. Ther be many Irishe men that goe about with counterfeate licenses; and if they perceiue you wil stryatly examen them, they will immediatly saye they can speake no Englishe.

¶ Farther, vnderstand for trouth that the worst and wickedst of all this beastly generation are scarse comparable to these prating Pallyardes. All for *the* most parte of these wil either lay to their legs an herb called Sperewort, eyther Arsnicke, which is called Ratesbane. The nature of this Spereworte wyll rayse a great blister in a night vpon the soundest part of his body; and if the same be taken away, it wyl dry vp againe and no harme. But this Arsnicke will so poyson the same legge or sore, that it will euer after be incurable: this do they for gaine and to be pitied. The most of these that walke about be Walchmen.

[1] Printed *this*

¶ A FRATER. Cap. 8.

Some of these Fraters will cary blacke boxes at their gyrdel, wher in they haue a briefe of the Queenes maiesties letters patentes, geuen to suche[1] poore spitlehouse for the reliefe of the poore there, whiche briefe is a coppie of the letters patentes, *and* vtterly fained, if it be in paper or in[2] parchment without the great scale. Also, if the same brief be in printe,[3] it is also of auctoritie. For the Printers wil sée *and* wel vnderstand, before it come in presse, that the same is lawfull. Also, I am credibly informed that the chiefe Proctors of manye of these houses, that seldome trauel abroad them selues, but haue their factors to gather for them, which looke very slenderly to the impotent and miserable creatures committed to their charge, *and* die for want of cherishing; wheras they *and* their wiues are wel crammed *and* clothed, *and* will haue of the best. And the founders of euery such house, or the chiefe of the parishe wher they be, woulde better sée vnto these Proctors, that they might do their duty, they should be wel spoken of here, and in the world to come abou*n*dantly therefore rewarded. I had of late an honest man, and of good wealthe, repayred to my house to common wyth me aboute certeyne affaires. I inuited the same to dinner, and dinner beinge done, I demaunded of hym some newes of these[4] parties were hee dwelte. "Thankes be to God, syr," (saith he); "all is well *and* good now." "Now!" (quoth I) "this same 'nowe' [leaf 13] declareth *that* some things of late hath not bene wel." "Yes, syr," (q*uoth* he) "the[5] matter is not great. I had thought I should haue bene wel beaten within this seuenth night." "How so?" (quoth I). "Mary, syr," sayd he, "I am Counstable for fault of a better, and was commaunded by the Iusticer to watch. The watch being set, I toke an honest man, one of my neighbors, with me, and went vp to the ende of the towne as far as the spittle house, at which house I heard a great noyse, and, drawing nere, stode close vnder the wall, and this was at one of the clocke after midnight.

---

[1] B. inserts *a*
[2] B. omits *in*
[3] Probably the reason why "in print" came to be considered synonymous with "correct." See 2 Gent. of Verona, act ii. sc. 1, 175.
[4] *those.* B.
[5] B. omits *the*

Where he harde swearinge, pratinge, and wagers laying, and the pot apase walkinge, and xl. pence gaged vpon a matche of wrastling, pitching of the barre, and casting of the sledge. And out they goe, in a fustian fume, into the backe syde, where was a great Axiltrye,[1] and there fell to pitching of the barre, being thre to thre. The Moone dyd shine bright, the Counstable with his neighboure myght see and beholde all that was done. And howe the wyfe of the house was rostinge of a Pyg, whyle her gestes were in their matche. At the laste they coulde not agree vpon a caste, and fell at wordes, and from wordes to blowes. The Counstable with his[2] fellowe runnes vnto them, to parte them, and in the partinge lyckes a drye blowe or two. Then the noyse increased; the Counstable woulde haue had them to[3] the stockes. The wyfe of the house runnes out with her goodman to intreat the Counstable for her gestes, and leaues the Pyg at the fyre alone. In commeth two or thrée of the next neighboures, beinge waked wyth this noise, and into the house they come, and fynde none therein, but the Pygge well rosted, and carieth the same awaye wyth them, spyte and all, with suche breade and drinke also as stoode vpon the table. When the goodman and the goodwyfe of the house hadde intreated and pacified the Counstable, shewinge vnto him that they were Proctors and Factores all of Spyttell houses, and that they taryed there but to breake theyr fast, and woulde ryde awaye immediatelye after, for they had farre to goe, and therefore mente to ryde so earlye. And comminge into their house agayne, fyndinge the Pygge wyth bread and drincke all gonne, made a greate exclamation, for they knewe not who had the same.

¶ The Counstable returning and hearinge the lamentable wordes of the good wyfe, howe she had lost both meate and drinke, and sawe it was so in deede, hée laughed in his sleue, and commaunded her to dresse no more at vnlawfull houres for any gestes. For hée thought it better bestowed vppon those smell feastes his poore neigh-

---

[1] Castynge of axtre & eke of ston,
Sofere hem þere to vse non;
Bal, and barres, and suche play,
Out of chycheȝorde put a-way.—
Myrc, p. 11, l. 334-7 (E. E. T. Soc. 1868)

[2] Printed *hts*

[3] *to to.* B.

boures then vppon suche sturdye Lubbares. The nexte mornynge betymes the [leaf 13, back] spitte and pottes were sette at the Spittle house doore for the owner. Thus were these Factours begyled of theyr breakefast, and one of them hadde well beaten an other; "And, by my trouth," (quoth thys Counstable) "I was gladde when I was well ryd of them." "Why," quoth I, "coulde the[y] caste the barre and sledge well?" "I wyll tell you, syr," (quoth hée) "you knowe there hath bene manye games this Sommer. I thinke verely, that if some of these Lubbars had bene there, and practysed amongest others, I beleue they woulde haue carryed awaye the beste games. For they were so stronge and sturdye, that I was not able to stande in their handes." "Well" (quoth I) "at these games you speake of, both legges and armes bée tryed." "Yea," quoth this offycer, "they bée wycked men. I haue séene some of them sithens wyth cloutes bounde aboute theyr legges, and haltynge wyth their staffe in their handes. Wherefore some of theym, by GOD, bee nought all."

¶ A ABRAHAM MAN. Cap. 9.

These Abrahom men be those that fayne themselues to haue beene mad, and haue bene kept eyther in Bethelem or in some other pryson a good tyme, *and* not one amongst twenty that euer came in pryson for any such cause: yet wyll they saye howe pitiously and most extreamely they haue bene beaten, and dealt with all. Some of these be merye and verye pleasant, they wyll daunce and sing; some others be as colde and reasonable to talke wyth all. These begge money; eyther when they come at Farmours howses they wyll demaunde Baken, eyther chéese, or wooll, or any thinge that is worthe money. And if they espye small company within, they wyll with fierce countenaunce demaund some what. Where for feare the maydes wyll geue theym largely to be ryd of theym.

¶ If they maye conuenyently come by any cheate, they wyl picke and steale, as the v[p]right man or Roge, poultrey or lynnen. And all wemen that wander bée at their commaundemente. Of all that euer I saw of this kynde, one naminge him selfe Stradlynge is the craftiest and moste dyssemblyngest Knaue.

Hée is able wyth hys tounge and vsage to deceaue and abuse the wysest man that is. And surely for the proporcion of his body, with euery member there vnto appertayninge, it cannot be a mended. But as the prouerbe is "God hath done his part." Thys Stradlyng sayth he was the Lord Sturtons man; and when he was executed, for very pensiuenes of mynde, [leaf 14] he fell out of his wytte, and so continued a yeare after and more; and that with the very gréefe and feare, he was taken wyth a marueilous palsey, that both head and handes wyll shake when he talketh, with anye and that a pase or fast, where by he is much pytied, and getteth greately. And if I had not demaunded of others, bothe men and women, that commonly walketh as he doth, and knowen by them his déepe dissimylation, I neuer hadde vnderstand the same. And thus I end wyth these kynde of vacabondes.

¶ A FRESHE WATER MARINER OR WHIPIACKE. Cap. 10.

THese Freshwater Mariners, their shipes were drowned in the playne of Salisbery. These kynde of Caterpillers counterfet great losses on the sea; these bée some Western men, and most bée Irishe men. These wyll runne about the countrey wyth a counterfet lycence, fayninge either shypwracke, or spoyled by Pyrates, neare the coaste of Cornwall or Deuonshyre, and set a lande at some hauen towne there, hauynge a large and formall wrytinge, as is aboue sayd, with the names and seales of suche men of worshyppe, at the leaste foure or fiue, as dwelleth neare or next to the place where they fayne their landinge. And neare to those shieres wyll they not begge, vntyll they come into Wylshyre, Hamshyre, Barkeshyre, Oxfordshyre, Harfordshyre, Middelsex, and so[1] to London, and downe by the ryuer to séeke for their shyppe and goods that they neuer hade: then passe they through Surrey, Sossex, by the sea costes, and so into Kent, demaunding almes to bring them home to their country.

¶ Some tyme they counterfet the seale of the Admiraltie. I haue diuers tymes taken a waye from them their lycences, of both sortes, wyth suche money as they haue gathered, and haue confiscated the same to the pouerty nigh adioyninge to me. And they wyll not

[1] Omitted in 1573.

beelonge with out another. For at anye good towne they wyll renewe the same. Once wyth muche threatninge and faire promises, I required to knowe of one companye who made their lycence. And they sweare that they bought the same at Portsmouth, of a Mariner there, and it cost them[1] two shillinges; with such warrantes to be so good and efectuall, that if any of the best men of lawe, or learned, aboute London, should peruse the same, they weare able to fynde no faute there with, but would assuredly allow the same.

him (sic). B.

These two pyctures, lyuely set out,
One bodye and soule, god send him more grace.
This mounstrous desembelar, a Cranke all about.
Vncomly couetinge, of eche to imbrace,
Money or wares, as he made his race.
And sometyme a marynar, and a saruinge man,
Or els an artificer, as he would fayne than.
Such shyftes he vsed, beinge well tryed,
A bandoninge labour, tyll he was espyed.
Conding punishment, for his dissimulation,
He sewerly receaued with much declination [2]

[1] This page is not in Bodley ed.   [2] 1573 reads *exclamation*

[leaf 15] ¶ A COUNTERFET CRANKE. Cap. 11.

THese that do counterfet the Cranke be yong knaues and yonge harlots, that depely dissemble the falling sicknes. For the Cranke in their language is the falling euyll. I haue séene some of these with fayre writinges testimoniall, with the names and seales of some men of worshyp in Shropshyre, and in other Shieres farre of, that I haue well knowne, and haue taken the same from them. Many of these do go without writinges, and wyll go halfe naked, and looke most pitiously. And if any clothes be geuen them, the[y][1] immediatly sell the same, for weare it they wyll not, because they would bée the more pitied, and weare fylthy clothes on their heades, and neuer go without a péece of whyte sope about them, which, if they sée cause or present gaine, they wyll priuely conuey the same into their mouth, and so worke the same there, that they wyll fome as it were a Boore, *and* maruelously for a tyme torment them selues ; and thus deceiue they the common people, and gayne much. These haue commonly their harlots as the other.

Apon Alhollenday in the morning last Anno domini. 1566, or my[2] booke was halfe printed, I meane the first impression, there came earely in the morninge a Counterfet Cranke vnder my lodgynge at the whyte Fryares, wythin the cloyster, in a lyttle yard or coorte, where aboutes laye two or thre great Ladyes, beyng without the lyberties of London, where by he hoped for the greatter gayne ; this Cranke there lamentably lamentinge and pitefully crying to be releued, declared to dyuers their hys paynfull and miserable dysease. I being rysen and not halfe ready, harde his dolfull wordes and rufull mornings, hering him name the falling sicknes, thought assuredlye to my selfe that hée was a depe desemblar ; so, comminge out at a sodayne, and beholdinge his vgly and yrksome attyre, hys lothsome and horyble countinance, it made me in a meruelous parplexite what to thinke of hym, whether it were fayned or trouth,—for after this manner went he : he was naked from the wast vpward, sauyng he had a old Ierken[3] of leather patched, and that was lose[4] about hym, that all his bodye laye out bare ; a filthy foule cloth he ware on his head,

[1] *they*. B. [2] *my my*. B. [3] *gyrken (et seqq.)*. B. [4] *loose*. B.

being cut for the purpose, hauing a narowe place to put out his face, with a bauer made to trusse vp his beard, and a stryng that tyed the same downe close aboute his necke; with an olde felt hat which he styll caried in his hande to receaue the charytye and deuotion of the people, for that woulde he hold out from hym; hauyng hys face, from the eyes downe ward, all smerd with freshe bloud, [leaf 15, back] as thoughe he had new falon, and byn tormented wyth his paynefull panges,—his Ierken beinge all be rayde with durte and myre, and hys hatte and hosen also, as thoughe hée hadde wallowed in the myre: sewerly the sighte was monstrous and terreble. I called hym vnto me, and demaunded of hym what he ayled. "A, good maister," quoth he, "I haue the greuous and paynefull dyseas called the falynge syckenes." "Why," quoth I, "howe commeth thy Ierken, hose, and hat so be rayd with durte and myre, and thy skyn also?" "A, good master, I fell downe on the backesyde here in the fowle lane harde by the watersyde; and there I laye all most all night, and haue bled all most all the bloude owte in my bodye." It raynde that morninge very fast; and whyle I was thus talkinge with hym, a honest poore woman that dwelt thereby brought hym a fayre lynnen cloth, and byd hym wype his face therewyth; and there beinge a tobbe standing full of rayne water, offered to geue hym some in a dishe that he might make hym selfe cleane: hée refuseth[1] the same. "Why dost thou so?" quoth I. "A, syr," sayth he, "yf I shoulde washe my selfe, I shoulde fall to bléedinge a freshe againe, and then I should not stop my selfe:" these wordes made me the more to suspecte hym.

Then I asked of hym where he was borne, what is name was, how longe he had this dysease, and what tyme he had ben here about London, and in what place. "Syr," saythe he, "I was borne at Leycestar, my name is Nycholas Genings,[2] and I haue had this falling sycknes viij. yeares, and I can get no remedy for the same; for I haue it by kinde, my father had it and my friendes before me; and I haue byne these two yeares here about London, and a yeare and a halfe in bethelem." "Why, wast thou out of thy wyttes?" quoth I. "Ye, syr, that I was."

[1] *refused*. B.   [2] *Gennins*. B.

"What is the Kepars name of the house?" "Hys name is," quoth hée, "Iohn Smith." "Then," quoth I, "hée must vnderstande of thy dysease; yf thou hadest the same for the tyme thou wast there, he knoweth it well." "Ye, not onely he, but all the house bée syde," quoth this Cranke ; "for I came thens but within this fortnight." I had stande so longe reasoning the matter wyth him that I was a cold, and went into my chamber and made me ready, and commaunded my seruant to repayre to bethelem, and bringe me true worde from the keper there whether anye suche man hath byn with him as a prisoner hauinge the dysease aforesayd, and gaue hym a note of his name and the kepars also: my seruant, retorninge to my lodginge, dyd assure me that neither was there euer anye such man there, nether yet anye keper of any suche name; but hée that was there keper, he sent me hys name in writing, affirming that hee letteth no man depart from hym vnlesse he be fet a waye by [leaf 16] hys fréendes, and that none that came from hym beggeth aboute the Citye. Then I sent for the Printar of this booke, and shewed hym of this dyssembling Cranke, and how I had sent to Bethelem to vnderstand the trouth[1], and what aunsweare I receaued againe, requiringe hym that I might haue some seruant of his to watche him faithfully that daye, that I might vnderstand trustely to what place he woulde repaire at night vnto, and thether I promised to goe my selfe to sée their order, and that I woulde haue hym to associate me thether: hée gladly graunted to my request, and sent two boyes, that both diligently and vygelantly accomplisht the charge geuen them, and found the same Cranke aboute the Temple, where about the most parte of the daye hée begged, vnlesse it weare about xii. of the clocke he wente on the backesyde of Clementes Ine without Temple barre: there is a lane that goeth into the Feldes; there hee renewed his face againe wyth freshe bloud, which he caried about hym in a bladder, and dawbed on freshe dyrte vpon his Ierken, hat, and hoson.

¶ And so came backe agayne vnto the Temple, and sometyme to the Watersyde, and begged of all that passed bye: the boyes behelde howe some gaue grotes, some syxe pens, some gaue more;

[1] *trough.* B.

for hée looked so ougleie and yrksomlye, that euerye one pytied his miserable case that bechelde hym. To bee shorte, there he passed all the daye tyll night approched; and when it began to bée some what dark, he went to the water syde and toke a Skoller,[1] and was sette ouer the Water into Saincte Georges feldes, contrarye to my expectatian; for I had thought he woulde haue gonne into Holborne or to Saynt Gylles in the felde; but these boyes, with Argues and Lynces eyes, set sewre watche vppon him, and the one tooke a bote and followed him, and the other went backe to tell his maister.

The boye that so folowed hym by Water, had no money to pay for his Bote hyre, but layde his Penner and his Ynkhorne to gage for a penny; and by that tyme the boye was sette ouer, his Maister, wyth all celeryte, hadde taken a Bote and followed hym apase: now hadde they styll a syght of the Cranke, wych crossed ouer the felddes towardes Newyngton, and thether he went, and by that tyme they came thether it was very darke: the Prynter hadde there no acquaintance, nether any kynde of weapon about hym, nether knewe he[2] how farre the Cranke woulde goe, becawse hee then suspected that they dogged hym of purposse; he there stayed hym, and called for the Counstable, whyche came forthe dylygentelye to inquyre what the matter was: thys zelous Pryntar charged thys offycer [leaf 16, back] wyth hym as a malefactor and a dessemblinge vagabonde — the Counstable woulde haue layde him all night in the Cage that stode in the streate. "Naye," saythe this pitifull Prynter, "I praye you haue him into your house; for this is lyke to be a cold nyght, and he is naked: you kepe a vytellinge house; let him be well cherished this night, for he is well hable to paye for the same. I knowe well his gaynes hath byn great to day, and your house is a sufficient pryson for the tyme, and we wil there serche hym. The Counstable agreed there vnto: they had him in, and caused him to washe him selfe: that donne, they demaunded what money he had about hym. Sayth this Cranke, "So God helpe me, I haue but xii. pence," and plucked oute the same of a lytle pursse. "Why, haue you no more?" quoth they. "No," sayth this Cranke, "as God shall saue my soule at the day of iudgement." "We must se more," quoth they,

---

[1] 1573 reads *skollocr* [2] Omitted in 1573 edit.

and began to stryp hym. Then he plucked out a nother purse, wherin was xl. pens. "Toushe," sayth[1] thys Prynter, "I must see more." Saythe this Cranke, "I pray God I bée dampned both body[2] and soule yf I haue anye more." "No," sayth thys Prynter, "thou false knaue, here is my boye that dyd watche thée all this daye, and sawe when such men gaue the péeses of sixe pens, grotes, and other money; and yet thou hast shewed vs none but small money." When thys Cranke hard this, and the boye vowinge it to his face, he relented, and plucked out another pursse, where in was eyght shyllings and od money; so had they in the hole that he had begged that day xiij. shillings iii. [3]pens halfepeny[3]. Then they strypt him starke naked, and as many as sawe him sayd they neuer sawe hansommer man, wyth a yellowe flexen beard[4], and fayre skynned, withoute anye spot or greffe. Then the good wyfe of the house fet her goodmans[5] olde clocke, and caused the same to be cast about him, because the sight shoulde not abash her shamefast maydens, nether loth her squaymysh sight.

Thus he set[6] downe at the Chemnes end, and called for a potte of Béere, and dranke of a quarte at a draft, and called for another, and so the thyrde, that one had bene sufficient for any resonable man, the Drynke was so stronge.[7] I my selfe, the next morninge, tasted thereof; but let the reader iudge what and howe much he would haue dronke and he had bene out of feare. Then when they had thus wrong water out of a flint in spoyling him of his euyl gotten goods, his passing pens[8], and fleting trashe, The printer with this offecer were in gealy gealowsit[9], and deuised to search a barne for some roges and vpright men, a quarter of a myle from the house, that stode a lone in the fieldes, and wente out about their businos, leauing this cranke alone with his wyfe and maydens: this crafty Cranke, espying al gon, requested the good wife that [leaf 17] hee might goe out on the backesyde to make water, and to exonerate his paunche: she bad hym drawe the lache of the dore and goe out, neither thinkinge or mistrusting he

---

[1] *sayih* (*sic*). B. [2] printed *dody* [3–3] *d. ob.* B. [4] *bede.* B.
[5] *mans.* B. [6] 1573 inserts *him ; sette hym.* B. [7] 1573 inserts *that*
[8] *pence.* B. [9] The 1573 edition reads *ioly ioylitie ; gelowsy.* B.

would haue gon awaye naked; but, to conclude, when hee was out, he cast awaye the cloke, and, as naked as euer he was borne, he ran away, ¹ that he could ² neuer be hard of ³ againe.¹ Now ³ the next morning betimes, I went vnto Newington, to vnderstand what was done, because I had word or it was day that there my printer was; and at my comming thether, I hard the hole circumstaunce, as I aboue haue wrytten; and I, seing the matter so fall out, tooke order with the chiefe of the parish that this xiij. shyllings *and* iij. ⁴ pens halfpeny⁴ might the next daye be equally distributed, by their good discrecions, to the pouertie of the same parishe,⁵ and so it was done.

¹ The 1573 edition finishes the sentence thus:—" ouer the fields to his own house, as hée afterwards said."
² *woulde.* B. ³⁻³ *again til now.* B. ⁴⁻⁴ *d. ob.* B.
⁵ The 1573 edition continues thus:—" wherof this crafty Cranke had part him selfe, for he had both house and wife in the same parishe, as after you shall heare. But this lewde lewterar could not laye his bones to labour, hauing got once the tast of this lewd lasy lyfe, for al this fayr admonition, but deuised other suttel sleights to maintaine his ydell liuing, and so craftely clothed him selfe in mariners apparel, and associated him self with an other of his companions: they hauing both mariners apparel, went abroad to aske charity of *th*e people, fayning they hadde loste their shippe with all their goods by casualty on the seas, wherewith they gayned much. This crafty Cranke, fearinge to be mistrusted, fell to another kinde of begging, as bad or worse, and apparelled himselfe very well with a fayre black fréese cote, a new payre of whyte hose, a fyne felt hat on his head, a shert of flaunders worke esteemed to be worth xvi. shillings; and vpon newe yeares day came againe into the whyt Fryers to beg: the printer, hauing occasion to go that ways, not thinking of this Cranke, by chaunce met with him, who asked his charitie for Gods sake. The printer, vewing him well, did mistrust him to be the counterfet Cranke which deceuied him vpon Alhollen daye at night, demaunded of whence he was and what was his name, ' Forsoth,' saith he, ' my name is Nicolas Genings, and I came from Lecester to séeke worke, and I am a hat-maker by my occupation, and all my money is spent, and if I coulde get money to paye for my lodging this night, I would seke worke to morowe amongst the hatters.' The printer perceiuing his depe dissimulation, putting his hand into his purse, seeming to giue him some money, and with fayre allusions brought him into the stréete, where he charged the constable with him, affirminge him to be the counterfet Cranke that ranne away vpon Alholon daye last. The constable being very loth to medle with him, but the printer knowing him and his depe disceit, desyred he mought be brought before the debutie of the ward, which straight was accomplished, which whe*n* he came before the debuty, he demaunded of him of whence he was and what was his name; he answered as before he did vnto *th*e printer: the debutie asked the printer what he woulde laye vnto hys charge; he answered and aleged him to be a vagabond and depe deceyuer of the people, and the counterfet Crank that ran away vpon Alhallon day last from the constable of Newington and him, and requested him earnestly to send him to ward: the debuty thinking him to be deceiued, but

¶ A DOMMERAR. Cap. 12.

THese Dommerars are leud and most subtyll people: the moste part of these are Walch men, and wyll neuer speake, vnlesse they haue extreame punishment, but wyll gape, and with a maruelous force wyll hold downe their toungs doubled, groning for your charyty, and holding vp their handes full pitiously, so that with their déepe dissimulation they get very much. There are of these many, *and* but one that I vnderstand of hath lost his toung in dede. Hauing on a time occasion to ride to Dartforde, to speake with a priest there, who maketh all kinde of conserues very well, and vseth stilling of waters; And repayringe to his house, I founde a Dommerar at his doore, and the priest him selfe perusinge his[1] lycence, vnder the scales and hands of certayne worshypfull men, had[2] thought the same to be good and effectuall. I taking the same writing, and neuerthelesse laid his commaundement vpon him, so that the printer should beare his charges if he could not iustifie it; he agreed thereunto. And so he and the constable went to cary him to the Counter; and as they were going vnder Ludgate, this crafty Cranke toke his héeles and ran down the hill as fast as he could dryve, the constable and the printer after him as fast as they coulde; but the printer of *the* twayn being lighter of fote, ouertoke him at fleete bridge, and with strong hand caried him to the counter, and safely deliuered him. In *the* morow *the* printer sent his boy that stripped him vpon Alhalon day at night to view him, because he would be sure, which boy knew him very well: this Crank confessed vnto the debuty, *that* he had hosted the night before in Kent stréet in Southwarke, at the sign of the Cock, which thing to be true, the printer sente to know, and found him a lyer; but further inquiring, at length found out his habitation, dwelling in maister Hilles rentes, hauinge a pretye house, well stuffed, with a fayre ioyne table, and a fayre cubbard garnished with peuter, hauing an old auncient woman to his wyfe. The printer being sure therof, repaired vnto the Counter, and rebuked him for his beastly behaviour, and told him of his false fayning, willed him to confesse it, and aske forgiuenes: he perceyued him to know his depe dissimulation, relented, and confessed all his disceit; and so remayning in the counter thrée dayes, was removed to Brydwel, where he was strypt starke naked, and his ougly attyre put vpon him before the maisters thereof, who wondered greatly at his dissimulation: for which offence he stode vpon the pillery in Cheapsyde, both in his ougly and handsome attyre. And after that went in the myll whyle his ougly picture was a drawing; and then was whypped at a cartes tayle through London, and his displayd banner caried before him vnto his own dore, and so backe to Brydewell again, and there remayned for a tyme, and at length let at libertie, on that condicio*n* he would proue an houest man, and labour truly to get his liuing. And his picture remayneth in Bridewell for a monyment."
—See, also, *post*, p. 89.

[1] *of his.* B.   [2] *which priest had.* B.

reading it ouer, and noting the scales, founde one of the scales like vnto a scale that I had aboute me, which scale I bought besides Charing crosse, that I was out of doubte it was none of those Gentlemens scales that had sub[s]cribed. And hauing vnderstanding before of their peuish practises, made me to conceaue that all was forged and nought. I made the more hast home; for well I wyst that he would and must of force passe through the parysh where I dwelt; for there was no other waye for hym. And comminge homewarde, I found them in the towne, accordinge to my expectation, where they were staid; for there was a Pallyarde associate with the Dommerar and partaker of his gaynes, whyche Pallyarde I sawe not at Dartford. The stayers of them was a gentleman called [1] *Chayne*, and a seruant of my Lord Kéepers, cald *Wostestowe*, which was [leaf 17, back] the chiefe causer of the staying of them, being a Surgien, *and* cunning in his science, had séene the lyke practises, and, as he sayde, hadde caused one to speake afore that was dome [2]. It was my chaunce to come at the begynning of the matter. "Syr," (quoth this Surgien) "I am bold here to vtter some part of my cunning. I trust" (quoth he) "you shall se a myracle wrought anon. For I once" (quoth he) "made a dumme man to speake." Quoth I, "you are wel met, and somwhat you haue preuented me; for I had thought to haue done no lesse or they hadde passed this towne. For I well knowe their writing is fayned, and they depe dissemblers." The Surgien made hym gape, *and* we could sée but halfe a toung. I required the Surgien to put hys fynger in his mouth, *and* to pull out his toung, and so he dyd, not withstanding he held strongly a prety whyle; at the length he pluckt out the same, to the great admiration of many that stode by. Yet when we sawe his tounge, hée would neither speake nor yet could heare. Quoth I to the Surgien, "knit two of his fyngers to gether, and thrust a stycke betwene them, and rubbe the same vp and downe a lytle whyle, and for my lyfe hée speaketh by and by." "Sir," quoth this Surgien, "I praye you let me practise and [3] other waye." I was well contented to sée the same. He had him into a house, and tyed a halter aboute the wrestes of his handes, and hoysed him vp ouer a beame, and

[1] *cal*. (*sic*). B.   [2] *dumme*. B.   [3] So printed. *an*. B.

there dyd let him hang a good while : at *the* length, for very paine he required for Gods sake to let him down. So he that was both deafe and dume coulde in short tyme both heare and speake. Then I tooke that money I could find in his pursse, and distributed the same to the poore people dwelling there, whiche was xv. pence halfepeny, being all that we coulde finde. That done, and this merry myracle madly made, I sent them with my seruaunt to the next Iusticer, where they preached on the Pyllery for want of a Pulpet, and were well whypped, and none dyd bewayle them.

¶ A DRONKEN TINCKAR. Cap. 13.

THese dronken Tynckers, called also Prygges, be beastly people, *and* these yong knaues be *the* wurst. These neuer go with out their Doxes, and yf their women haue anye thing about them, as apparell or lynnen, that is worth the selling, they laye the same to gage, or sell it out right, for bene bowse at their bowsing ken. And full sone wyll they bée wearye of them, and haue a newe. When they happen one woorke at any good house, their Doxes lynger alofe, and tarry for them in some corner ; and yf he taryeth longe from her, then she knoweth [leaf 18] he hath worke, and walketh neare, and sitteth downe by him. For besydes money, he looketh for meate and drinke for doinge his dame pleasure. For yf she haue thrée or foure holes in a pan, hee wyll make as many more for spedy gaine. And if he se any old ketle, chafer, or pewter dish abroad in the yard where he worketh, hée quicklye snappeth the same vp, and in to the booget it goeth round. Thus **they lyue with deceite.**

¶ I was crediblye informed, by such as could well **tell, that** one of these tipling Tinckers *with* his dogge robbed by the high way iiij. Pallyards and two Roges, six persons together, and tooke from them aboue foure pound in ready money, *and* hide him after in a thicke woode a daye or two, and so escaped vntaken. Thus with picking and stealing, mingled with a lytle worke for a coulour, they passe their time.

¶ A SWADDER, OR PEDLER. Cap. 14.

THese Swadders and Pedlers bee not all euyll, but of an indifferent behauiour. These stand in great awe of the vpright men, for they haue often both wares and money of them. But for as much as they séeke gayne vnlawfully against the lawes and statutes of this noble realme, they are well worthy to be registred among the number of vacabonds; and vndoubtedly I haue hadde some of them brought before me, when I was in commission of the peace, as malefactors, for bryberinge and stealinge. And nowe of late it is a greate practes of the vpright man, when he hath gotten a botye, to bestowe the same vpon a packefull of wares, and so goeth a time for his pleasure, because he would lyue with out suspition.

¶ A IARKE MAN, AND A PATRICO. Cap. 15.

FOR as much as these two names, a Iarkeman and a Patrico, bée in the old briefe of vacabonds, and set forth as two kyndes of euil doers, you shall vnderstande that a Iarkeman hathe his name of a Iarke, which is a seale in their Language, as one should make writinges and set seales for lycences and pasporte[1]. And for trouth there is none that goeth aboute the countrey of them that can eyther wryte so good and fayre a hand, either indite so learnedly, as I haue sene *and* handeled a number of them: but haue the same made in good townes where they come, as what can not be hadde for money, as the prouerbe sayth ("*Omnia venalia Rome*"), and manye hath confessed the same to me. [leaf 18, back] Now, also, there is a Patrico, and not a Patriarcho[2], whiche in their language is a priest that should make mariages tyll death dyd depart; but they haue none such, I am well assured; for I put you out of doubt that not one amo[n]gest a hundreth of them are maried, for they take lechery for no sinne, but naturall fellowshyp and good lyking loue: so that I wyll not blot my boke with these two that be not.

[1] *pasportes.* B.   [2] *Patriarch.* B.

¶ A DEMAUNDER FOR GLYMMAR. Cap. 16.

These Demaunders for glymmar be for the moste parte wemen; for glymmar, in their language, is fyre. These goe with fayned[1] lycences and counterfayted wrytings, hauing the hands and seales of suche gentlemen as dwelleth nere to the place where they fayne them selues to haue bene burnt, and their goods consumed with fyre. They wyll most lamentable[2] demaunde your charitie, *and* wyll quicklye shed salte teares, they be so tender harted. They wyll neuer begge in that Shiere where their losses (as they say) was. Some of these goe with slates at their backes, which is a shéete to lye in a nightes. The vpright men be very familiare with these kynde of wemen, and one of them helpes an other.

¶ A Demaunder for glymmar came vnto a good towne in Kente, to ask the charitie of the people, hauinge a fayned lycens aboute her that declared her misfortune by fyre, donne in Somerset shyre, walkinge with a wallet on her shoulders, where in shée put the deuotion of suche as hadde no money to geue her; that is to saye, Malte, woll, baken, bread, and cheese; and alwayes, as the same was full, so was it redye money to her, when she emptyed the same, where so euer shee trauelede: thys harlot was, as they terme it, snowte fayre, and had an vpright man or two alwayes attendinge on her watche (whyche is on her parson), and yet so circumspecte, that they woulde neuer bee séene in her company in any good towne, vnlesse it were in smale vyllages where typling houses weare, eyther trauelinge to gether by the hygh wayes; but *the* troth is, by report, she would wekely be worth vi. or seuen shyllinges with her begging and bycherye. This glimmering Morte, repayringe to an Ine in *the* sayde towne where dwelt a wydow of fyftie wynter olde of good welth; but she had an vnthryftye sonne, whom she vsed as a chamberlaine to attend gestes when they repared to her house: this amerous man, be holdinge with ardante eyes thys[3] glymmeringe glauncer, was presentlye pyteouslye persed to the hart, and lewdlye longed to bée clothed vnder her lyuerye; and bestowinge [leaf 19] a

---

[1] *faynen*. B.   [2] *lamentably*. B.
[3] *beholding this*. B.

fewe fonde wordes with her, vnderstode strayte that she woulde be easlye perswaded to lykinge lechery, and as a man mased, mused howe to attayne to his purpose, for [1] he hadde no money. Yet consideringe wyth hym selfe that wares woulde bée welcome where money wanted, hée went with a wannion to his mothers chamber, and there sekinge aboute for odde endes, at length founde a lytle whystell of syluer that his mother dyd vse customablye to weare on, and had forgot the same for haste that morninge, and offeres the same closely to this manerly marian, that yf she would mete hym on the backesyde of the towne and curteously kys him with out constraynt, she shoulde bée mystres thereof, and it weare much better. "Well," sayth she, "you are a wanton;" and beholdinge the whystell, was farther in loue there with then rauysht wyth his person, and agred to mete him presently, and to accomplyshe his fonde fancy:—to be short, and not tedyous, a quarter of a myle from the towne, he merely toke measure of her vnder a bawdye bushe; so she gaue hym that she had not, and he receiued that he coulde not; and taking leue of eche other with a curteous kysse, she plesantly passed forth one her iornaye, *and* this vntoward lycorous chamberlayne repayred home warde. But or these two tortylles tooke there leue, the good wyfe myssed her whystell, and sent one of her maydenes in to her chamber for the same, and being long sawght for, none coulde be founde; her mystres hering that, diligent search was made for the same; and that it was taken awaye, began to suspecte her vnblessed babe, and demaunded of her maydens whether none of them sawe her sonne in her chamber that morning, and one of them aunswered that she sawe him not there, but comming from thens: then had she ynough, for well she wyste that he had the same, and sent for him, but he could not be founde. Then she caused her hosteler, in whome she had better affyaunce in for his trouth,—and yet not one amongst twenty of them but haue well left there honesty, (As I here a great sorte saye)—to come vnto her, whiche attended to knowe her pleasure. "Goe, seke out," saythe she, "my vntowarde sonne, and byd hym come speake with me." "I sawe him go out," saythe he, "halfe an houre

[1] *but.* B.

sithens one the backesyde. I hadde thought you hadde sent him of your arrante." "I sent him not," quoth she; "goe, loke him out."

¶ This hollowe hosteler toke his staffe in his necke, and trodged out apase that waye he sawe him before go, and had some vnderstanding, by one of the maydens, that his mistres had her whistell stolen *and* suspected her sonne; and he had not gone farre but that he espyed him comming homeward alone, and, meting him, axed where he had ben. [leaf 19. back] "Where haue I bene?" q*uoth* he, and began to smyle. "Now, by the mas, thou hast bene at some baudy banquet." "Thou hast euen tolde trouth," q*uoth* thys chamberlayne. "Sewerly," q*uoth* this hosteler, "thou haddest the same woman that begged at our house to day, for *the* harmes she had by fyre: where is she?" q*uoth* he. "She is almost a myle by this tyme," q*uoth* this chamberlayne. "Where is my mystres whystell?" quoth this hosteler; "for I am well assured that thou haddest it, and I feare me thou hast geuen it to that harlot." "Why! is it myssed?" quoth this chamberlayne. "Yea," q*uoth* this hosteler, and shewed him all the hole circumstaunce, what was both sayde and thought on him for the thing. "Well, I wyl tell the," quoth this Chamberlayne. "I wylbe playne with the. I had it in dede, and haue geue*n* the same to this woman, and I praye the make the best of it, and helpe nowe to excuse the matter, and yet surely and thou wouldest take so much payne for me as to ouer take her, (for she goeth but softly, and is not yet farre of) and take the same from her, and I am euer thyne assured fréende." "Why, then, go with me," quoth this hostler. "Nay, in faythe," quoth this Chamberlayne; "what is frear then gift? and I hadde prety pastime for the same." "Hadest thou so?" quoth this hosteler; "nowe, by the masse, and I wyll haue some to, or I wyll lye in the duste or I come agayne." Passing with hast to ouer take this paramoure, within a myle from *th*e place where he departed he ouertoke her, hauing an vpright man in her company, a stronge and a sturdye vacabond: some what amased was this hosteler to se one familiarly in her company, for he had well hopped to haue had some delycate dalyance, as his fellowe hadde; but, seinge the matter so fallout, and being of

good corage, and thinking to him selfe that one true man was better
then two false knaues, and being on the high way, thought vpon
helpe, if nede had bene, by such as had passed to and fro, Demaunded fersely the whistell that she had euyn nowe of his fellowe.
"Why, husband," quoth she, "can you suffer this wretche to
slaunder your wyfe?" "A vaunt verlet," quoth this vpright man,
and letes dryue with all his force at this hosteler, and after halfe [1]
a dosen blowes, he strycks his staffe out of his hande, and as this
hosteler stept backe to haue taken vp his staffe agayne, his glymmeringe Morte flinges a great stone at him, and strake him one the heade
that downe hee fales, wyth the bloud about his eares, and whyle hée
laye this amased, the vpright man snatches awaye his pursse, where
in hée hadde money of his mystresses as well as of his owne, and
there let him lye, and went a waye with spede that they were neuer
harde of more. When this drye beaten hosteler was come to him
selfe, hée fayntlye wandereth home, and crepethe in to hys couche,
and restes [leaf 20] his ydle heade: his mystres harde that hée was
come in, and layde him downe on his beade, repayred straight vnto
him, and aske hym what he ayled, and what the cause was of his so
sudden lying one his bed. "What is the cause?" quoth this
hosteler; "your whystell, your whistel,"—speaking the same
pyteouslye thre or foure tymes. "Why, fole," quoth his mystrisse,
"take no care for that, for I doe not greatly waye it; it was worth
but thrée shyllinges foure pens." "I would it had bene burnt for
foure yeares agon." "I praye the why so," quoth his mystres; "I
think thou art mad." "Nay, not yet," quoth this hosteler, "but I
haue bene madly handlyd." "Why, what is the matter?" quoth
his mystres, and was more desirous to know the case. "*And* you
wyl for geue my fellowe and me, I wyll shewe you, or els I wyll
neuer doe it." Shée made hym presently faithfull promisse that shée
woulde. "Then," saythe hee, "sende for your sonne home agayne,
whyche is ashamed to loke you in the face." "I agre there to,"
sayth shée. "Well, then," quoth this hosteler, "youre sonne hathe
geuen the same Morte that begged here, for the burninge of her
house, a whystell, and you haue geuen her v. shyllinges in money,

[1] Omitted in 1573

and I haue geuen her ten shyllinges of my owne." "Why, howe so?" quoth she. Then he sadly shewed her of his myshap, with all the circumstaunce that you haue harde before, and howe hys pursse was taken awaye, and xv. shyllinges in the same, where of v. shyllinges was her money and x. shyllinges his owne money. "Is this true?" quoth his mystres. "I, by my trouth," quoth this hosteler, "and nothing greues me so much, neyther my beating, neither the losse of my money, as doth my euell *and* wreched lucke." "Why, what is the matter?" quoth his mystres. "Your sonne," saythe this hosteler, "had some chere and pastyme for that whystell, for he laye with her, and I haue bene well beaten, and haue had my pursse taken from me, and you knowe your sonne is merrye and pleasaunt, and can kepe no great councell; and then shall I bemocked *and* loughed to skorne in all places when they shall here howe I haue bene serued." "Nowe, out vpon you knaues both," quoth his mystres, and laughes oute the matter; for she well sawe it would not other wyse preuayle.

¶ A BAWDY BASKET. Cap. 17.

THese Bawdy baskets be also wemen, and go with baskets and Capcases on their armes, where in they haue laces, pynnes, nedles, white ynkell, and round sylke gyrdles of al coulours. These wyl bye conneyskins,[1] *and* steale linen clothes of on hedges. And for their trifles they wil procure of mayden seruaunts, when [leaf 20, back] their mystres or dame is oute of the waye, either some good peece of beefe, baken, or ch.ese, that shalbe worth xij. pens, for ii. pens of their toyes. And as they walke by the waye, they often gaine some money wyth their instrument, by such as they sodaynely mete withall. The vpright men haue good acquayntance with these, and will helpe and relieue them when they want. Thus they trade their lyues in lewed lothsome lechery. Amongest them all is but one honest woman, and she is of good yeares; her name is Ione Messenger. I haue had good proofe of her, as I haue learned by the true report of diuers.

[1] Rabbitskins

There came to my gate the last sommer, Anno Domini .1566, a very miserable man, and much deformed, as burnt in the face, blere eyde, and lame of one of his legges that he went with a crouche. I axed him wher he was borne, and where he dwelt last, and shewed him that thether he must repaire and be releued, and not to range aboute the countrey; and seing some cause of cherytie, I caused him to haue meate and drinke, and when he had dronke, I demaunded of him whether he was neuer spoyled of the vpright man or Roge. "Yes, that I haue," quoth he, "and not this seuen yeres, for so long I haue gon abroad, I had not so much taken from me, and so euyll handeled, as I was within these iiij. dayes." "Why, how so?" quoth I. "In good fayth, sir," quoth hée, "I chaunced to méete with one of these bawdy baskets which had an vpright man in her company, and as I would haue passed quietly by her, 'man,' sayth she vnto vnto her make, 'do you not se this ylfauored, windshaken knaue?' 'Yes,' quoth the vpright man; 'what saye you to him?' 'this knaue[1] oweth me ii. shyllings for wares that [2] he had of me, halfe a yere a go, I think it well.' Sayth this vpright man, 'syra,' sayth he, 'paye your dets.' Sayth this poore man, 'I owe her none, nether dyd I euer bargane with her for any thinge, and as this[3] aduysed I neuer sawe her before in all my lyfe.' 'Mercy, god!' quoth she, 'what a lyinge knaue is this, and he wil not paye you, husband, beat him suerly,' and the vpright man gaue me thre or foure blowes on my backe and shoulders, and would haue beat me worsse and I had not geuen hym all the money in my pursse, and in good fayth, for very feare, I was fayne to geue him xiiij. pens, which was all the money that I had. 'Why,' sayth this bawdy basket, 'hast thou no more? then thou owest me ten pens styll; and, be well assured that I wyll bée payde the next tyme I méete with thée.' And so they let me passe by them. I praye god saue and blesse me, and al other in my case, from such wycked persons," quoth this poore man. "Why, whether went they then?" quoth I. "Into east Kent, for I mete with them on thyssyde of Rochester. I haue dyuers tymes bene attemted, but

---

[1] B. inserts *sayth she*.   [2] Omitted in 1573.   [3] 1573 reads *I am*

I neuer loste [leaf 21] much before. I thanke god, there came styll company by a fore this vnhappy time." "Well," quoth I, "thanke God of all, and repaire home into thy natyue countrey."

¶ A AUTEM MORT. Cap. 18.

THese Autem Mortes be maried wemen, as there be but a fewe. For Autem in their Language is a Churche; so she is a wyfe maried at the Church, and they be as chaste as a Cowe I haue, *that* goeth to Bull euery moone, with what Bull she careth not. These walke most times from their husbands companye a moneth and more to gether, being asociate with another as honest as her selfe. These wyll pylfar clothes of hedges: some of them go with children of ten or xii. yeares of age ; yf tyme and place serue for their purpose, they wyll send them into some house, at the window, to steale and robbe, which they call in their language, Milling of the ken; and wil go wit*h* wallets on their shoulders, and slates at their backes. There is one of these Autem Mortes, she is now a widow, of fyfty yeres old ; her name is Alice Milson : she goeth about with a couple of great boyes, the yongest of them is fast vpon xx. yeares of age ; and these two do lye with her euery night, and she lyeth in the middes : she sayth that they be her children, that beteled be babes borne of such abhominable bellye.

¶ A WALKING MORT. Cap. 19.

THese walkinge Mortes bee not maryed : these for their vnhappye yeares doth go as a Autem Morte, and wyll saye their husbandes died eyther at Newhauen, Ireland, or in some seruice of the Prince. These make laces vpon staues, *and* purses, that they cary in their hands, and whyte vallance for beddes. Manye of these hath hadde and haue chyldren : when these get ought, either with begging, bychery, or brybery, as money or apparell, they are quickly shaken out of all by the vpright men, that they are in a maruelous feare to cary any thinge aboute them that is of any valure. Where fore, this pollicye they vse, they leaue their money now with one and then with a nother trustye housholders, eyther with the good man or good wyfe, some tyme in one shiere, and then in another, as they trauell: this haue I knowne, *that* iiij. or v. shyllinges, yea x. shyllinges, lefte in a place, and the same wyll they come for againe within one quarter of a yeare, or some tyme not in halfe a yeare; and all this is to lytle purpose, for all their peuyshe [leaf 21, back] pollycy; for when they bye them lynnen or garmentse, it is taken awaye from them, and worsse geuen them, or none at all.

¶ The last Sommer, Anno domini .1566, being in familiare talke with a walking Mort that came to my gate, I learned by her what I could, and I thought I had gathered as much for my purpose as I desired. I began to rebuke her for her leud lyfe and beastly behauor, declaring to her what punishment was prepared and heaped vp for her in the world to come for her fylthy lyuinge and wretched conuersation. "God helpe," q*uoth* she, "how should I lyue? none wyll take me into seruice; but I labour in haruest time honestly." "I thinke but a whyle with honestie," q*uoth* I. "Shall I tell you," q*uoth* she, "the best of vs all may be amended; but yet, I thanke god, I dyd one good dede within this twelue monthes." "Wherein?" q*uoth* I. Sayth she, "I woulde not haue it spoken of agayne." "Yf it be méete and necessary," quod I, "it shall lye vnder my feete." "What meane you by that?" quoth she. "I meane," q*uod* I, "to hide the same, and neuer to discouer it to any." "Well," q*uoth* she, and began to laugh as much as she could, and sweare by the masse that if I disclosed the same to any, she woulde neuer more[1] tell me any thinge. "The last sommer," q*uoth* she, "I was greate with chylde, and I traueled into east kent by the sea coste, for I lusted meruelously after oysters and muskels[2], and gathered many, and in *the* place where I found them, I opened them and eate them styll: at the last, in seking more, I reached after one, and stept into a hole, and fel in into the wast, and their dyd stycke, and I had bene drowned if the tide had come, and espyinge a man a good waye of, I cried as much as I could for helpe. I was alone, he hard me, and repaired as fast to me as he might, and finding me their fast stycking, I required for gods sake his helpe; and whether it was with stryuinge and forcing my selfe out, or for ioye I had of his comminge to me, I had a great couller in my face, and loked red and well

---

[1] Omitted in 1573.   [2] *mussels.* B.

coullered. And, to be playne with you, hée lyked me so well (as he saydⅽ) that I should there lye styll, and I would not graunt him, that he might lye with me. And, by my trouth, I wist not what to answeare, I was in such a perplexite; for I knew the man well: he had a very honest woman to his wyfe, and was of some welth; and, one the other syde, if I weare not holpe out, I should there haue perished, and I graunted hym that I would obeye to his wyll: then he plucked me out. And because there was no conuenient place nere hande, I required hym that I might go washe my selfe, and make me somewhat clenly, and I would come to his house and lodge all night in his barne, whether he mighte repaire to me, and accomplyshe hys desire, 'but let it not be,' quoth she,[1] 'before nine of the clocke at nyghte [leaf 22] for then there wylbe small styrring. And I may repaire to the towne,' quoth she,[2] 'to warme and drye my selfe'; for this was about two of the clocke in the after none. 'Do so,' quoth hée; 'for I must be busie to looke oute my cattell here by before I can come home.' So I went awaye from hym, and glad was I." "And why so?" quoth I. "Because," quoth she, "his wyfe, my good dame, is my very fréend, and I am much beholdinge to her. And she hath donne me so much good or this, that I weare loth nowe to harme her any waye." "Why," quoth I, "what and it hadde béene any other man, and not your good dames husbande?" "The matter had bene the lesse," quoth shée. "Tell me, I pray the," quoth I, "who was the father of thy chylde?" She stodyd a whyle, and sayde that it hadde a father. "But what was hée?" quoth I. "Nowe, by my trouth, I knowe not," quoth shée; "you brynge me out of my matter so, you do." "Well, saye on," quoth I. "Then I departed strayght to the towne, and came to my dames house, And shewed her of my mysfortune, also of her husbands vsage, in all pointes, and that I showed her the same for good wyll, and byde her take better héede to her husbande, and to her selfe: so shée gaue me great thankes, and made me good chéere, and byd me in anye case that I should be redye at the barne at that tyme and houre we had apoynted; 'for I knowe well,' quoth this good wyfe, 'my husband wyll not breake wyth the. And one thinge I warne[3] the, that thou

[1] *he*, ed. 1573.   [2] *I*, ed. 1573.   [3] *warrant*. B.

geue me a watche worde a loud when hée goeth aboute to haue his pleasure of the, and that shall¹ bée " fye, for shame, fye," and I wyll bée harde by you wyth helpe. But I charge the kéepe thys secret vntyll all bee fynesed ; and holde,' saythe thys good wyfe, ' here is one of my peticotes I geue thée.' ' I thanke you, good dame,' quoth I, ' and I warrante you I wyll bée true and trustye vnto you.' So my dame lefte me settinge by a good fyre with meate and drynke ; and wyth the oysters I broughte with me, I hadde greate cheere : shée wente strayght and repaired vnto her gossypes dwelling there by ; and, as I dyd after vnderstande, she made her mone to them, what a naughtye, lewed, lecherous husbande shée hadde, and howe that she coulde not haue hys companye for harlotes, and that she was in feare to take some fylthy dysease of hym, he was so commen a man, hauinge lytle respecte whome he hadde to do with all ; ' and,' quoth she, ' nowe here is one at my house, a poore woman that goeth aboute the countrey that he woulde haue hadde to doe withall ; wherefore, good neyghboures and louinge gossypes, as you loue me, and as you would haue helpe at my hand another tyme, deuyse some remedy to make my husband a good man, *th*at I may lyue in some suerty without disease, and that hée may saue his soule that God so derelye [leaf 22, back] bought.' After shée hadde tolde her tale, they caste their persinge eyes all vpon her, but one stoute dame amongst the rest had these wordes—' As your pacient bearinge of troubles, your honest behauiour among vs your neyghbours, your tender and pytifull hart to the poore of the parysh, doth moue vs to lament your case, so the vnsatiable carnalite of your faithelesse husbande doth instigate and styre vs to deuyse and inuent some spéedy redresse for your ease² and the amendement of hys lyfe. Wherefore, this is my councell and you wyll bée aduertysed by me ; for³ I saye to you all, vnlesse it be this good wyfe, who is chéefely touched in this matter, I haue the nexte cause ; for hée was in hande wyth me not longe a goe, and companye had not bene present, which was by a meruelous chaunce, he hadde, I thinke, forced me. For often hée hath bene tempering⁴ with me, and yet haue I sharpely sayde him

¹ *should*. B.   ² 1573 reads *case*   ³ Omitted in 1573.
⁴ 1573 reads *tempting*

naye: therefore, let vs assemble secretly into the place where hée hathe apuynted to méete thys gyllot that is at your house, and lyrke preuelye in some corner tyll hée begyn to goe aboute his busines. And then me thought I harde you saye euen nowe that you had a watche word, at which word we wyll all stepforth, being fiue of vs besydes you, for you shalbe none because it is your husbande, but gette you to bed at your accustomed houre. And we wyll cary eche of vs[1] good byrchen rodde in our lappes, and we will all be muffeled for knowing, and se that you goe home and acquaynt that walking Morte with the matter; for we must haue her helpe to hold, for alwaies foure must hold and two lay one.' 'Alas!' sayth this good wyfe, 'he is to stronge for you all. I would be loth, for my sake you should receaue harme at his hande.' 'feare you not,' quoth these stout wemen, 'let her not geue the watch word vntyl his hosen be abaut his legges. And I trowe we all wylbe with him to bring before he shall haue leasure to plucke them vp againe.' They all with on voyce ag[r]ed to the matter, that the way she had deuised was the best: so this good wife repaired home; but before she departed from her gossypes, she shewed them at what houre they should preuely come in on *the* backsid, *and* where to tary their good our: so by *the* time she came in, it was all most night, and found the walking Morte still setting by the fyre, and declared to her all this new deuyse aboue sayd, which promised faythfully to full fyll to her small powre as much as they hadde deuysed: within a quarter of an oure after, in commeth the good man, who said that he was about his cattell. "Why, what haue we here, wyfe, setting by the fyre? *and* yf she haue eate and dronke, send her into the barne to her lodging for this night, for she troubeleth the house." "Euen as you wyll husbande," sayth his wyfe; "you knowe she commeth once in two yeres into these [leaf 23] quarters. Awaye," saythe this good wyfe, "to your lodginge." "Yes, good dame," sayth she, "as fast as I can:" thus, by loking one[2] on the other, eche knewe others mynde, and so departed to her comely couche: the good man of the house shrodge hym for Ioye, thinking to hym selfe, I wyll make some pastyme with you anone. And calling to his wyfe for hys sopper, set

---

[1] B. inserts *a*   [2] *won.* B.

him downe, and was very plesant, and dranke to his wyfe, *and* fell to his mammerings, and mounched a pace, nothing vnderstanding of the bancquet that[1] was a preparing for him after sopper, *and* according to the prouerbe, that swete meate wyll haue sowre sawce : thus, when he was well refreshed, his sprietes being reuyued, entred into familiare talke with his wife, of many matters, how well he had spent that daye to both there proffytes, sayinge some of his cattell[2] were lyke to haue bene drowned in the dyches, dryuinge others of his neyghbours cattell out that were in his pastures, *and* mending his fences that were broken downe. Thus profitably he had consumed the daye, nothinge talking of his helping out of the walkinge Morte out of the myre, nether of his request nor yet of her[3] promisse. Thus feding her w*ith* frendly fantacyes, consumed two houres and more. Then fayninge howe hée would se in what case his horse were in and howe they were dressed, Repaired couertly into the barne, where as his frée[n]dlye foes lyrked preuely, vnlesse it were this manerly Morte, that comly couched on a bottell of strawe. "What, are you come?" q*uoth* she; "by the masse, I would not for a hundreth pound that my dame should knowe that you were here, eyther any els of your house." "No, I warrant the," sayth this good man, "they be all safe and fast ynough at their woorke, and I wylbe at mine anon." And laye downe by her, and strayght would haue had to do w*ith* her. "Nay, fye," sayth she, "I lyke not this order: if ye lye with me, you shall surely vntrus you *and* put downe your hosen, for that way is most easiest and best." "Sayest thou so?" quoth he, "now, by my trouth agred." And when he had vntrussed him selfe and put downe, he began to assalt the vnsatiable[4] fort "Why," quoth she, that was with out shame, sauinge for her promes, "And are you not ashamed?" "neuer a whyte," sayth he, "lye downe quickely." "Now, fye, for shame, fye," sayth shée a loude, whyche was the watche word. At the which word, these fyue furious, sturdy, muffeled gossypes flynges oute, and takes sure holde of this be trayed parson, sone[5] pluckinge his hosen downe lower, and byndinge the same fast about his féete ;

---

[1] B. omits *that*   [2] B. inserts *that*   [3] 1573 reads *his*
[4] B. reads *vnsanable*, or *vnsauable*   [5] 1573 reads *some*

then byndinge his handes, and knitting a hande charcher about his eyes, that he shoulde not sée; and when they had made hym sure and fast, Then they layd him one vntyll they weare windles. "Be good," sayth this Morte, "vnto my maister, for the passion of God," [leaf 23, back] and layd on as fast as the rest, and styll seased not to crye vpon them to bée mercyfull vnto hym, and yet layde on a pace; and when they had well beaten hym, that the bloud braste plentifullye oute in most places, they let hym lye styll bounde. With this exhortation, that he shoulde from that tyme forth knowe his wyfe from other mens, and that this punishment was but a flebyting in respect of that which should followe, yf he amended not his manners. Thus leuynge hym blustering, blowing, and fominge for payne, and malyncolye that hée neither might or coulde be reuenged of them, they vanyshed awaye, and hadde thys Morte with them, and safely conuayde her out of the towne: sone after commeth into the barne one of the good mans boyes, to fet some haye for his horse. And fyndinge his maister lyinge faste bounde and greuouslye beaten with rodes, was sodenly abashed and woulde haue runne out agayne to haue called for helpe; but his maister bed hym come vnto hym and vnbynd hym; "and make no wordes," quoth he, "of this. I wylbe reuenged well inoughe;" yet not with standinge, after better aduyse, the matter beinge vnhonest, he thought it meter to let the same passe, and, not, as the prouerbe saythe, to awake the sleping dogge. "And, by my trouth," quoth this walkinge Morte, "I come nowe from that place, and was neuer there sythens this parte was playde, whiche is some what more then a yeare. And I here a very good reporte of hym now, that he loueth his wyfe well, and vseth hym selfe verye honestlye; and was not this a good acte? nowe, howe saye you?" "It was pretely handeled," quoth I, "and is here all?" "Yea," quoth she, "here is the ende."

¶ A Doxe. Cap. 20.

THese Doxes be broken and spoyled of their maydenhead by the vpright men, and then they haue their name of Doxes, and not afore. And afterwarde she is commen and indifferent for any that wyll vse her, as *homo* is a commen name to all men. Such as be fayre and some what handsome, kepe company with the walkinge Mortes, and are redye alwayes for the vpright men, and are cheifely mayntayned by them, for others shalbe spoyled for their sakes: the other, inferior, sort wyll resorte to noble mens places, and gentlemens houses, standing at the gate, eyther lurkinge on the backesyde about backe houses, eyther in hedge rowes, or some other thycket, expectinge their praye, which is for the vncomely company of some curteous gest, of whome they be refreshed with meate and some money, where eschaunge is made, ware for ware: this bread and meate they vse to carrye in their [leaf 24] greate hosen; so that these beastlye brybinge[1] bréeches serue manye tymes for bawdye purposes. I chaunced, not longe sithens, familiarly to commen with a Doxe that came to my gate, and surelye a pleasant harlot, and not so pleasant as wytty, and not so wytty as voyd of all grace and goodnes. I founde, by her talke, that shée hadde passed her tyme lewdlye eyghttene yeares in walkinge aboute. I thoughte this a necessary instrument to attayne some knowledge by; and before I woulde grope her mynde, I made her both to eate and drynke well; that done, I made her faythfull promisse to geue her some money, yf she would open and dyscouer to me such questions as I woulde demaunde of her, and neuer to bée wraye her, neither to disclose her name. "And you shoulde," sayth she, "I were vndon:" "feare not that," quoth I; "but, I praye the," quoth I, "say nothing but trouth." "I wyll not," sayth shée. "Then, fyrste tell me," quoth I, "how many vpright men and Roges dost thou knowe, or hast thou knowne and byn conuersaunt with, and what their names be?" She paused a whyle, and sayd, "why do you aske me, or wherefore?" "For nothinge els," as I sayde, "but that I woulde knowe them when they came to my gate." "Nowe, by my trouth" (quoth she) "then are yea neuer the neare, for all myne acquayntaunce, for the moste parte, are deade." "Dead!" quoth I, "howe dyed they, for wante of cherishinge, or of paynefull diseases?" Then she sighed, and sayde they were hanged. "What, all?" quoth I, "and so manye walke abroade, as I dayelye see?" "By my trouth," quoth she, "I

[1] *bryberinge*. B.

knowe not paste six or seuen by their names," and named the same to me. " When were they hanged?" quoth I. " Some seuen yeares a gone, some thrée yeares, and some wit*h*in this fortnight," and declared the place where they weare executed, which I knewe well to bée true, by the report of others. " Why " (quoth I) " dyd not this sorrowfull and fearefull sight much greue the, and for thy tyme longe and euyll spent?" " I was sory," quoth shée, " by the Masse; for some of them were good louing men. For I lackt not when they had it, and they wanted not when I had it, and diuers of them I neuer dyd forsake, vntyll the Gallowes departed vs." " O, mercyfull God!" quoth I, and began to blesse me. " Why blesse ye?" quoth she. " Alas! good gentleman, euery one muste haue a lyuinge." Other matters I talked of; but this nowe maye suffice to shewe the Reader, as it weare in a glasse, the bolde beastly lyfe of these Doxes. For suche as hath gone anye tyme abroade, wyll neuer forsake their trade, to dye therefore. I haue hadde good profe thereof. There is one, a notorious harlot, of this affinitye, called Besse Bottomelye; she hath but one hande, and she hath murthered two children at the least.

[leaf 24, back]   ¶ A Dell. Cap. 21.

A Dell is a yonge wenche, able for generation, and not yet knowen or broken by the vpright man. These go abroade yong, eyther by the death of their parentes, and no bodye to looke vnto them, or els by some sharpe mystres that they serue, do runne away out of seruice; eyther she is naturally borne one, and then she is a wyld Dell: these are broken verye yonge; when they haue béene lyen with all by the vpright man, then they be Doxes, and no Dels. These wylde dels, beinge traded vp with their monstrous mothers, must of necessytie be as euill, or worsse, then their parents, for neither we gather grapes from gréene bryars, neither fygs from Thystels. But such buds, such blosoms, such euyll sede sowen, wel worsse beinge growen. .

¶ A Kynchin Morte. Cap. 22.

Kynching Morte is a lytle Gyrle: the Mortes their mothers carries them at their backes in their slates, whiche is their shetes, and bryngs them vp sauugely[1], tyll they growe to be rype, and soone rype, soone rotten.

¶ A Kynchen Co. Cap. 23.

A Kynchen Co is a young boye, traden vp to suche peuishe purposes as you haue harde of other young ympes before, that when he groweth vnto yeres, he is better to hang then to drawe forth.

¶ Their vsage in the night. Cap. 24.

Now I thinke it not vnnecessary to make the Reader vnderstand how and in what maner they lodge a nights in barnes or backe houses, and of their vsage there, for asmuch as I haue acquaynted them with their order and practises a day times. The arche and chiefe walkers that hath walked a long time, whose experience is great, because of their continuinge practise, I meane all Mortes and Doxes, for their handsomnes and diligence for making of their couches. The men neuer trouble them selues with *that* thing, but takes the same to be the dutye of *the* wyfe. And she shuffels vp a quayntitye of strawe or haye into some pretye carner of the barne [leaf 25] where she maye conuenientlye lye, and well shakethe the same, makinge the heade some what hye, and dryues the same vpon the sydes and fete lyke abed: then she layeth her wallet, or some other lytle pack of ragges or scrype vnder her heade in the strawe, to beare vp the same, and layethe her petycote or cloke vpon and ouer the strawe, so made lyke a bedde, and that serueth for the blancket. Then she layeth her slate, which is her sheete, vpon that; and she haue no shéete, as fewe of them goo without, then she spreddeth some large cloutes or rags ouer the same, and maketh her ready, and layeth her drouselye downe. Many wyll plucke of their smockes, and laye the same vpon them in stede of their vpper shéete, and all her other pelte and

---

[1] B. reads *safely*

trashe vpon her also; and many lyeth in their smockes. And if the
rest of her clothes in colde weather be not sufficient to kepe her
warme, then she taketh strawe or haye to performe the matter. The
other sorte, that haue not slates, but toumble downe and couche a
hogshead in their clothes, these bée styll lousye, and shall neuer be
with out vermyn, vnlesse they put of theire clothes, and lye as is a
boue sayde. If the vpright man come in where they lye, he hath
his choyse, and crepeth in close by his Doxe: the Roge hath his
leauings. If the Morts or Doxes lye or be lodged in some Farmers
barne, and the dore be ether locked or made fast to them, then wyl
not the vpright man presse to come in, Vnles it be in barnes and
oute houses standinge alone, or some distance from houses, which be
commonly knowne to them, As saint Quintens, thrée Cranes of the
vintrey, Saynt Tybbes, and Knapsbery. These foure be with in one
myle compasse neare vnto London. Then haue you iiij. more in
Middlesex, drawe the pudding out of the fyre in Harrow on the hyll
parish, *th*e Crose Keyes in Cranford[1] parish, Saynt Iulyans in
Thystell worth parish, the house of pyty in Northhall parysh. These
are their chiefe houses neare about London, where commonly they
resorte vnto for Lodginge, and maye repaire thether freelye at all
tymes. Sometyme shall come in some Roge, some pyckinge knaue,
a nymble Prygge; he walketh in softly a nightes, when they be at
their rest, and plucketh of as many garmentes as be ought worth that
he maye come by, and worth money, and maye easely cary the same,
and runneth a waye with the same with great seleritye, and maketh
porte sale at some conuenient place of theirs, that some be soone
ready in the morning, for want of their Casters *and* Togema*n*s.
Where in stéede of blessinge is cursing; in place of praying, pestelent
prating with odious othes *and* terrible threatninges. The vpright
men haue geuen all these nycke names to the places aboue sayde.
Y[e]t haue [leaf 25, back] we two notable places in Kent, not fare
from London : the one is betwene Detforde and Rothered, called the
Kynges barne, standing alone, that they haunt commonly; the other
is Ketbroke, standinge by blacke heath, halfe a myle from anye
house. There wyll they boldlye drawe the latche of the doore, and

[1] 1573 reads *Crayford*.

go in when the good man with hys famyly be at supper, and syt downe without leaue, and eate and drinke with them, and either lye in the hall by the fyre all night, or in *the* barne, if there be no rome in the house for them. If the doore be eyther bolted or lockt, if it be not opened vnto them when they wyl, they wyl breake the same open to his farther cost. And in this barne sometyme do lye xl. vpright men with their Doxes together at one time. And this must the poore Farmer suffer, or els they threaten him to burne him, and all that he hath.

THE NAMES OF THE VPRIGHT MEN, ROGES, AND PALLYARDS.

HEre followeth the vnrulye rablement of rascals, and the moste notoryous and wyckedst walkers that are lyuinge nowe at this present, with their true names as they be called and knowne by. And although I set and place here but thre orders, yet, good Reader, vnderstand that all the others aboue named are deriued and come out from the vpright men and Roges. Concerning the number of Mortes and Doxes, it is superfluous to wryte of them. I could well haue don it, but the number of them is great, and woulde aske a large volume.

¶ Upright Men.

A.[1]	D.	E.
Antony Heymer.	Dowzabell skylfull in fence.	Edmund Dun, a singing man.
Antony Iackeson.	Dauid Coke.	Edward Skiner, *alias* Ned Skiner.
B.	Dycke Glouer.	
Burfet.	Dycke Abrystowe.	Edward Browne.
Bryan medcalfe.	Dauid Edwardes.	F.
C.	Dauid Holand.	Follentine Hylles.
Core the Cuckold.	Dauid Iones.	Fardinando angell.
Chrystouer Cooke.		Fraunces Dawghton.

[1] The arrangement in Bodley ed. is not alphabetical.

G.

Gryffin.
Great Iohn Graye.
George Marrinar.
George Hutchinson.

H.

Hary Hylles, alias Harry godepar.
[leaf 26] Harry Agglyntine.
Harry Smyth, he driueleth when he speaketh.
Harry Ionson.

I.

Iames Barnard.
Iohn Myllar.
Iohn Walchman.
Iohn Iones.
Iohn Teddar.
Iohn Braye.
Iohn Cutter.
Iohn Bell.
Iohn Stephens.
Iohn Graye.
Iohn Whyte.
Iohn Rewe.
Iohn Mores.
Iohn a Farnando.
Iohn Newman.
Iohn Wyn, alias Wylliams.
Iohn a Pycons.
Iohn Tomas.
Iohn Arter.
Iohn Palmer, alias Tod.

Iohn Geffrey.
Iohn Goddard.
Iohn Graye the lytle.
Iohn Graye the great.
Iohn Wylliams the Longer.
Iohn Horwood, a maker of wels; he wyll take halfe his bargayne in hand, *and* when hée hath wrought ii. or iii. daies, he runneth away with his earnest.
Iohn Peter.
Iohn Porter.
Iohn Appowes.
Iohn Arter.
Iohn Bates.
Iohn Comes.
Iohn Chyles, *alias* great Chyles.
Iohn Leuet; he maketh tappes and fausets.
Iohn Louedall, a maister of fence.
Iohn Louedale.
Iohn Mekes.
Iohn Appowell.
Iohn Chappell.
Iohn Gryffen.
Iohn Mason.
Iohn Humfrey, with the lame hand.
Iohn Stradling, with the shaking head.
Iohn Franke.
Iohn Baker.
Iohn Bascafeld.

K.

L.

Lennard Iust.
Long Gréene.
Laurence Ladd.
Laurence Marshall.

M.

N.

Nicolas Wilson.
Ned Barington.
Ned Wetherdon.
Ned holmes.

O.

P.

Phyllype Gréene.

Q.

R.

Robart Grauener.
Robart Gerse.
Robart Kynge.
Robart Egerton.
Robart Bell, brother to Iohn Bell.
Robart Maple.
Robart Langton.
Robyn Bell.
Robyn Toppe.
Robart Brownswerd, he werith his here long.
Robart Curtes.
Rychard Brymmysh.
Rychard Iustyce.
Rychard Barton.

Rychard Constance.
Rychard Thomas.
Rychard Cadman.
Rychard Scategood.
Rychard Apryce.
Rychard Walker.
Rychard Coper.

S.

Steuen Neuet.

T.

Thomas Bulloke. [leaf 20, back]
Thomas Cutter.
Thomas Garret.
Thomas Newton.
Thomas Web.

Thomas Graye, his toes be gonne.
Tom Bodel.
Thomas Wast.
Thomas Dawson *alias* Thomas Iacklin.
Thomas Basset.
Thomas Marchant.
Thomas Web.
Thomas Awefeld.
Thomas Gybbins.
Thomas Lacon.
Thomas Bate.
Thomas Allen.

V.

W.

Welarayd Richard.

Wylliam Chamborne.
Wylliam Pannell.
Wylliam Morgan.
Wylliam Belson.
Wylliam Ebes.
Wylliam Garret.
Wylliam Robynson.
Wylliam Vmberuile.
Wylliam Dauids.
Wyll Pen.
Wylliam Iones.
Wyll Powell.
Wylliam Clarke.
Water Wirall.
Wylliam Browne.
Water Martyne.[1]
Wylliam Grace.
Wylliam Pyckering.

ROGES.

A.

Arche Dowglas, a Scot.

B.

Blacke Dycke.

C.

D.

Dycke Durram.
Dauid Dew neuet, a counterfet Cranke.

E.

Edward Ellys.
Edward Anseley.

F.

G.

George Belberby.
Goodman.
Gerard Gybbin, a counterfet Cranke.

H.

Hary Walles, with the lytle mouth.
Humfrey ward.
Harry Mason.

I.

Iohn Warren.
Iohn Donne, with one legge.

Iohn Elson.
Iohn Raynoles, Irysh man.
Iohn Harrys.
Iames Monkaster, a counterfet Cranke.
Iohn Dewe.
Iohn Crew, with one arme.
Iohn Browne, great stamerar.

L.

Lytle Dycke.
Lytle Robyn.
Lambart Rose.

[1] Omitted in 1573 edit.

M.

More, burnt in the hand.[1]

N.

Nicholas Adames, a great stamerar.[2]

Nycholas Crispyn.

Nycholas Blunt *alias* Nycholas Gennings, a counterfet Cranke.

Nycholas Lynch.

R.

Rychard Brewton.

Rychard Horwod, well nere lxxx. yeares olde; he wyll byte a vi. peny nayle a sonder with his téeth, and a bawdye [leaf 27] dronkard.

Richard Crane; he carieth a Kynchne Co at his backe.

Rychard Iones.

Raffe Ketley.

Robert Harrison.

S.

Simon Kynge.

T.

Thomas Paske.

[3]Thomas Bere.

Thomas Shawnean, Irish man.

Thomas Smith, with the skald skyn.[3]

W.

Wylliam Carew.

Wylliam wastfield.

Wylson.

Wylliam Gynkes, with a whyte bearde, a lusty and stronge man; he runneth about the countrey to séeke worke, with a byg boy, his sonne carying his toles as a dawber or playsterer, but lytle worke serueth him.

¶ PALLYARDS.

B.

Bashford.

D.

Dycke Sehan Irish.

Dauid Powell.

Dauid Iones, a counterfet Crank.

E.

Edward Heyward, hath his Morte following him, which fained the Cranke.

Edward Lewes, a dummerer.

H.

Hugh Iones.

I.

Iohn Perse,[4] a counterfet Cranke.

Iohn dauids.

Iohn Harrison.

Iohn Carew.

Iames Lane, with one eye, Irish.

Iohn Fysher.

Iohn Dewe.

Iohn Gylford, Irish, with a counterfet lisence.

L.

Laurence with the great legge.

N.

Nycholas Newton, carieth a fained lisence.

Nicholas Decase.

---

[1] Omitted in 1573 ed.   [2] Last three words omitted in 1573 ed.
[3] The 1573 ed. arranges these names in the following order:—
   Thomas Béere.
   Irish man.
   Thomas Smith with the skalde skin.
   Thomas Shawneam.
[4] The 1573 ed. reads *Persk*

P.	Richard Thomas.	Thomas Dauids.
Prestoue.		Wylliam Thomas.
R.	S.	Wylliam Coper with the Harelyp.
Robart Lackley.	Soth gard.	
Robart Canloke.	Swanders.	Wyll Pettyt, beareth a Kinchen mort at his back.
Richard Hylton, caryeth ii. Kynchen mortes about him.	T.	
	Thomas Edwards.	Wylliam Bowmer.

There is aboue an hundreth of Irish men and women that wander about to begge for their lyuing, that hath come ouer within these two yeares. They saye the[y] haue béene burned and spoyled by the Earle of Desmond, and report well of the Earle of Vrmond.

¶ All these aboue wryten for the most part walke about Essex, Myddlesex, Sussex, Surrey, and Kent. Then let the reader iudge what number walkes in other Shieres, I feare me to great a number, if they be well vnderstande.

[leaf 27, back]   [1]Here followyth their pelting speche.[1]

Ere I set before the good Reader the leud, lousey language of these lewtering Luskes *and* lasy Lorrels, where with they bye and sell the common people as they pas through the countrey. Whych language they terme Peddelars Frenche, a vnknowen toung onely, but to these bold, beastly, bawdy Beggers, and vaine Vacabondes, being halfe myngled with Englyshe, when it is famyliarlye talked, and fyrste placinge thinges by their proper names as an Introduction to this peuyshe spéeche.

Nab, a head.	a pratling chete, a tounge.	quaromes, a body.
Nabchet, a hat or cap.	Crashing chetes, téeth.	prat, a buttocke.
Glasyers, eyes.	Hearing chetes, eares.	stampes, legges.
a smelling chete, a nose.	fambles, handes.	a caster, a cloke.
gan, a mouth.	a fambling chete, a rynge on thy hand.	a togeman, a cote.

[1] B. omits.

a commission,
  a shierte.
drawers,
  hosen.
stampers,
  shooes.
a mofling chete,
  a napkyn.
a belly chete,
  an apern.
dudes,
  clothes.
a lag of dudes,
  a bucke of clothes.
a slate or slates,
  a shéete or shetes.
lybbege,
  a bed.
bunge,
  a pursse.
lowre,
  monye.
mynt,
  golde.
a bord,
  a shylling.
halfe a borde,
  sixe pence.
flagg,
  a groate.
a wyn,
  a penny.
a make,
  a halfepeny.
bowse,
  drynke.
bene,
  good.
benshyp,
  very good.

quier,
  nought.
a gage,
  a quarte pot.
a skew,
  a cuppe.
pannam,[1]
  bread.
cassan,
  chéese.
yaram,[2]
  mylke.
lap,
  butter milke or whey.
[leaf 28] pek,
  meate.
poppelars,
  porrage.
ruff pek,
  baken.
a grunting chete or a patricos kynchen,
  a pyg.
a cakling chete,
  a cocke or capon.
a margery prater,
  a hen.
a Roger or tyb of the buttery,
  a Goose.
a quakinge chete or a red shanke,
  a drake or ducke.
grannam,
  corne.
a lowhinge chete,
  a Cowe.
a bletinge chete,
  a calfe or shéepe

a prauncer,
  a horse.
autem,
  a church.
Salomon,
  a alter or masse.
patrico,
  a priest.
nosegent,
  a Nunne.
a gybe,
  a writinge.
a Iarke,
  a seale.
a ken,
  a house.
a staulinge ken,
  a house that wyll receaue stolen ware.
a bousing ken,
  a ale house.
a Lypken,
  a house to lye in.
a Lybbege,
  a bedde.
glymmar,
  fyre.
Rome bouse,
  wyne.
lage,
  water.
a skypper,
  a barne.
strommell,
  strawe.
a gentry cofes ken,
  A noble or gentlemans house.
a gygger,
  a doore.

---

[1] The 1573 ed. reads *Yannam*
[2] B. reads *yarum*. The 1573 ed. reads *Param*

bufe,
 a dogge.
the lightmans,
 the daye.
the darkemans,
 the nyght.
Rome vyle,
 London.
dewse a vyle,
 the countrey.
Rome mort,
 the Quene.
a gentry cofe,
 a noble or gentleman.
a gentry morte,
 A noble or gentle woman.
the quyer cuffyn,[1]
 the Iusticer of peace.
the harman beck,
 the Counstable.
the harmans,
 the stockes.
Quyerkyn,
 a pryson house.
Quier crampringes,
 boltes or fetters.
tryninge,
 hanginge.
chattes,
 the gallowes.

the hygh pad,
 the hygh waye.
the ruffmans,
 the wodes or bushes.
a smellinge chete,
 a garden or orchard.
crassinge chetes,
 apels, peares, or anye other frute.
to fylche, to beate, to stryke, to robbe.[2]
to nyp a boung,
 to cut a pursse.
To skower the cramp-rings, [leaf 28, back]
 to weare boltes or fetters.
to heue a bough,
 to robbe or rifle a boeweth.
to cly the gerke,
 to be whypped.
to cutte benle,[3]
 to speake gently.
to cutte bene whydds,
 to speake or geue good wordes.
to cutte quyre whyddes,
 to geue euell wordes or euell language.
to cutte,
 to saye.

to towre,
 to sée.
to bowse,
 to drynke.
to maunde,
 to aske or requyre.
to stall,
 to make or ordaine.
to cante,
 to speake.
to myll a ken,
 to robbe a house.
to prygge,
 to ryde.
to dup the gyger,
 to open the doore.
to couch a hogshead,
 to lye downe and sléepe.
to nygle,
 to haue to do with a woman carnally.
stow you,
 holde your peace.
bynge a waste,
 go you hence.
to the ruffian,
 to the deuell.
the ruffian cly the,
 the deuyll take thée.

¶ The vpright Cofe canteth to the Roge.[4]

The vpright man speaketh to the Roge.

VPRIGHTMAN.[5]

Bene Lightmans to thy quarromes, in what lipken hast thou lypped in this darkemans, whether in a lybbege or in the strummell?

---

[1] *custyn.* B.
[2] For these two lines printed in small type, the 1573 edition reads,
 To fylche
  to robbe
[3] *benie.* B.   [4] *Roger.* B.   [5] *man.* B.

God morrowe to thy body, in what house hast thou lyne in all night, whether in a bed, or in the strawe?

ROGE.

I couched a hogshead in a Skypper this darkemans.
I layd[1] me downe to sléepe in a barne this night.

VPRIGHT MAN.[2]

I towre the strummel trine vpon thy nabchet[3] *and* Togman.
I sée the strawe hang vpon thy cap and coate.

ROGE.

I saye by the Salomon I will lage it of with a gage of benebouse; then cut to my nose watch.

I sweare by the masse[4], I wull washe it of with a quart of good drynke; [leaf 29][5] then saye to me what thou wylt.

MAN. Why, hast thou any lowre in thy bonge to bouse?
    Why, hast thou any money in thy purse to drinke?

ROGE. But a flagge, a wyn, and a make.
    But a grot, a penny, and a halfe penny.

MAN. Why, where is the kene that hath the bene bouse?
    where is the house that hath good drinke?

ROGE. A bene mort hereby at the signe of the prauncer.
    A good wyfe here by at the signe of the hors.

MAN. I cutt it is quyer buose, I bousd a flagge the laste dark mans.
    I saye it is small and naughtye drynke. I dranke a groate there the last night.

ROGE. But bouse there a bord, *and* thou shalt haue beneship.
    But drinke there a shyllinge, and thou shalt haue very good.

Tower ye yander is the kene, dup the gygger, and maund that is bene shyp.
    Se you, yonder is the house, open the doore, and aske for the best.

---

[1] *laye.* B.   [2] B. omits *vpright*.   [3] *nabches.* D.
[4] *masst.* B.   [5] This leaf is supplied in MS. in Mr Huth's edition.

MAN. This bouse is as benshyp[1] as rome bouse.
    This drinke is as good as wyne.

Now I tower that bene bouse makes nase nabes.
    Now I se that good drinke makes a dronken heade.

Maunde of this morte what bene pecke is in her ken.
    Aske of this wyfe what good meate shee hath in her house.

ROGE. She hath a Cacling chete, a grunting chete, ruff Pecke, cassan, and popplarr of yarum.
    She hath a hen, a pyg, baken, chese and mylke porrage.

MAN. That is beneshyp to our watche.
    That is very good for vs.

Now we haue well bousd, let vs strike some chete.
    Nowe we haue well dronke, let us steale some thinge.

Yonder dwelleth a quyere cuffen, it were beneship to myll hym.
    Yonder dwelleth a hoggeshe and choyrlyshe man, it were very well donne to robbe him.

ROGE. Nowe bynge we a waste to the hygh pad, the ruffmanes is by.
    Naye, let vs go hence to the hygh waye, the wodes is at hand.

MAN. So may we happen on the Harmanes, and cly the Iarke, or to the quyerken and skower quyaer cramprings, and so to tryning on the chates.
    [leaf 29, back] So we maye chaunce to set in the stockes, eyther be whypped, eyther had to prison house, and there be shackled with bolttes and fetters, and then to hange on the gallowes.

Gerry gan, the ruffian clye thee.
    A torde in thy mouth, the deuyll take thee.

MAN. What, stowe your bene, cofe, and cut benat whydds, and byng we to rome vyle, to nyp a bong; so shall we haue lowre for the bousing ken, and when we byng back to the deuseauyel, we wyll fylche some duddes of the Ruffemans, or myll the ken for a lagge of dudes.
    What, holde your peace, good fellowe, and speake better wordes, and go we to London, to cut a purse; then shal we haue money for the ale house, and

---

[1] *good* in the 1573 ed.

when wee come backe agayne into the country, wee wyll steale some lynnen clothes of one[1] hedges, or robbe some house for a bucke of clothes.

¶ By this lytle ye maye holy and fully vnderstande their vntowarde talke and pelting speache, mynglede without measure; and as they haue begonne of late to deuyse some new termes for certien thinges, so wyll they in tyme alter this, and deuyse as euyll or worsse. This language nowe beinge knowen and spred abroade, yet one thinge more I wyll ad vnto, not meaninge to Englyshe the same, because I learned the same[2] of a shameles Doxe, but for the phrase of speche I set it forth onely.

There was a proude patrico and a nosegent, he tooke his Iockam in his famble, and a wappinge he went, he dokte the Dell, hee pryge to praunce, he byngd a waste into the darke mans, he fylcht the Cofe, with out any fylch man.

Whyle this second Impression was in printinge, it fortuned that Nycholas Blunte, who called hym selfe Nycholan Gennyns, a counterefet Cranke, that is spoken of in this booke, was fonde begging in the whyte fryers on Newe yeares day last past, Anno domini .1567, and commytted vnto a offescer, who caried hym vnto the depetye of the ward, which commytted hym vnto the counter; *and as* the counstable and a nother would haue caried hym thether, This counterfet Cranke ran awaye, but one lyghter of fote then the other ouer toke hym, *and* so leading him to the counter, where he remayned three days, *and* from thence to Brydewell, where before the maister[3] he had his dysgysed aparell put vpon hym, which was monstrous to beholde, And after stode in Chepesyde with the same apparil on a scafold.[4]

A Stockes to staye sure, and safely detayne, [leaf 30]
Lasy lewd Leutterers, that lawes do offend,
Impudent persons, thus punished with payne,
Hardlye for all this, do meane to amende.

[1] The 1573 ed. has *some*
[2] Instead of "the same," the 1573 ed. reads *that*
[3] *maisters*. B.
[4] This paragraph is omitted in the ed. of 1573; but see note, *ante*, p. 56.

Fetters or shackles serue to make fast,
Male malefactours, that on myschiefe do muse,
Vntyll the learned lawes do quite or do cast,
Such suttile searchers, as all euyll do vse.

A whyp is a whysker, that wyll wrest out blood, [lf 30, bk]
Of backe and of body, beaten right well.
Of all the other it doth the most good,
Experience techeth, and they can well tell.

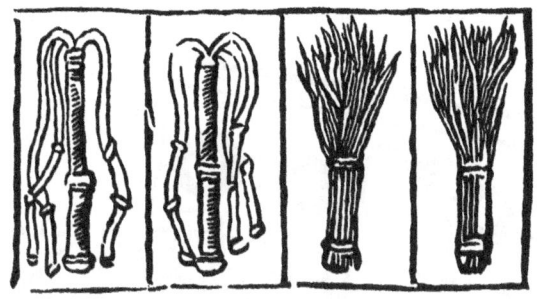

¶ O dolefull daye! nowe death draweth nere,
Hys bytter styng doth pearce me to the harte.

I take my leaue of all that be here,
Nowe piteously playing this tragicall parte.
Neither stripes nor teachinges in tyme could conuert,
wherefore an ensample let me to you be,
And all that be present, nowe praye you for me.

[1] ¶ This counterfet Cranke, nowe vew and beholde,
Placed in pyllory, as all maye well se:
This was he, as you haue hard the tale tolde,
before recorded with great suttylte,
Ibused manye with his inpiete,
his lothsome attyre, in most vgly manner,
was through London caried with dysplayd banner.[2]

---

[1] B. omits this stanza and has inserted the following lines under the cut.
This is the fygure of the counterfet Cranke, that is spoken of in this boke of Roges, called Nycholas Blunt other wyse Nycholas Gennyngs. His tale is in the xvii. lefe [pp. 55-6] of this booke, which doth showe vnto all that reades it, woundrous suttell and crafty deseit donne of *and* by him.

[2] This verse is omitted in the edition of 1573; also the wood-cut preceding it.

☞ Thus I conclude my bolde Beggars booke,
That all estates most playnely maye see,
As in a glasse well pollyshed to looke,
Their double demeaner in eche degree.
Their lyues, their language, their names as they be,
That with this warning their myndes may be warmed,
To amend their mysdeedes, and so lyue vnharmed.

FINIS.

¶ Imprinted at London, in Fletestrete, at the signe of the Faulcon by Wylliam gryffith.   Anno Domni. 1567.[1]

---

[1] B. adds 'the eight of January'. (This would make the year 1568 according to the modern reckoning. Harman's 'New Yeares day last past, Anno domini 1567', p. 86, must also be $156\frac{7}{8}$.)

A Sermon in Praise of Thieves and Thievery.

[*Lansdowne MS.* 98, *leaf* 210.]

A sermon made by Parson Haben vppon a mold hill at Hartely Row,[1] at the Comaundment of vij. theves, whoe, after they had robbed him, Comaunded him to Preache before them.

I Marvell that euerye man will seme to dispraise theverye, and thinke the doers thereof worthye of Death, when it is a thinge that Cometh nere vnto vertve, and is vsed of all men, of all sort*es* and in all countryes, and soe comaunded and allowed of god himselfe which thinge, because I cannot soe sapiently shewe vnto you a[2] soe shorte a tyme and in soe shorte a place, I shall desire you, gentle theves, to take in good p*ar*te this thinge that at this tyme Cometh to minde, not misdoubtinge but you of yo*ur* good knowledge are able to ad more vnto the same then this which I at this tyme shall shewe vnto you. ffirst, fortitude and stoutnes, Courage, and boldnes of stomacke, is Compted of some a vertue; which beinge graunted, Whoe is he then that will not Iudge theves vertuous, most stoute, most hardye? I most, withoute feare. As for stealinge, that is a thinge vsuall :—whoe stealeth not? ffor not only you that haue besett me, but many other in many places. Men, Woemen, *and* Children, Riche and poore, are dailye of that facultye, As the hange

---

[1] MS Rew. Hartley Row is on the South-Western road past Bagshot. The stretch of flat land there was the galloping place for coaches that had to make up time.

[2] *in*

A Sermon in Praise of Thieves and Thievery.

[*MS. Cott. Vesp.* A xxv. *leaf* 53.]

A sermon of parson Hyberdyne which he made att the commandemente of certen theves, after thay had Robbed hym, besydes hartlerowe, in hamshyer, in the feldes, ther standinge vpon a hyll where as a wynde myll had bene, in the presens of the theves that robbed hym, as followithe.

the sermon as followethe

I greatly mervell that any man wyll presume to dysprase theverie, and thynke the dooeres therof to be woorthy of deathe, consyderinge itt is a thynge that cumithe nere vnto vertue, beinge vsed of many in all contries, And commendid and allowed of god hym selfe; the which thinge, by-cause I cannot compendiously shew vnto yow at soo shorte a warnynge and in soo sharpe a wether, I shall desyer yow, gentle audiens of theves, to take in good parte thes thynges that at thys tyme cumythe to my mynde, not mysdowtynge but that yow of yowre good knowledge are able to add mutch more vnto ytt then this which I shall nowe vtter vnto yow. ffyrst, fortitude, and stowtnes of corage, and also bowldnes of minde, is commendyd of sume men to be a vertue; which, beinge grawnted, who is yt then that wyll not iudge theves to be vertused? for thay be of all men moste stowte and hardy, and moste withowte feare; for thevery is a thynge moste vsuall emonge all men, for not only yow that be here presente, but many other in dyuerse places, bothe men and wemen and chyldren, rytche and poore, are dayly of thys facultye,

man of Tiborne can testifye. That it is allowed of god himselfe, it is euident in many storyes of the Scriptures. And if you liste to looke in the whole Course of the bible, you shall finde that theves haue bin belovid of god. ffor Iacobe, when he Came oute of Mesopotomia, did steale his vncles lambes; the same Iacobe stale his brother Esawes blessinge; and that god saide, "I haue chosen Iacob and refused Esawe." The Children of Isarell, when they came oute of Egippe, didd steale the Egippsians Iewells and ring*es*, and god comaunded the[m] soe to doe. David, in the dayes of Ahemel[e]ch the preiste, came into the temple and stole awaye the shewe bread; And yet god saide, "this is a man accordinge to myne owne harte." Alsoe Christe himsellfe, when he was here vppon earth, did take an asse, a Colte, which was none of his owne. And you knowe that god saide, "this is my nown*e* sone, in whome I delighte."

Thus maye you see that most of all god delighteth in theves. I marvell, therefore, that men can despise yo*ur* lives, when that you are in all poynts almost like vnto Christe; for Christ hade noe dwellinge place,—noe more haue you. Christe, therefore, at the laste, was laide waite for in all places,—and soe are you. Christe alsoe at the laste was called for,—and soe shall you be. He was condemned,—soe shall you be. Christe was hanged,—soe shall you be. He descended into hell,—so shall you. But in one pointe you differ. He assendid into heaven,—soe shall you never, without gods mercye, Which god graunte for his mercyes sake! Toe whome, with the so*n*ne and the holye goste, be all hono*ur* and glory for euer and euer. Amen!

> After this good sermon ended, which Edefied them soe muche, Theye hadd soe muche Compassion on him, That they gave him all his mony agayne, and vij s more for his sermon.

as the hangman of tyboorne can testyfye: and that yt is allowed of god hym selfe, as it is euydente in many storayes of [the] scriptures; for yf yow looke in the hole cowrse of the byble, yow shall fynde that theves haue bene beloued of gode; for Iacobe, whan he came owte of Mesopotamia, dyd steale his vncle labanes kyddes; the same Iacobe also dyd steale his brothe[r] Esaues blessynge; *and* yett god sayde, "I haue chosen Iacobe *and* refused Esau." The chyldren of ysraell, whan they came owte of Egypte, dyd steale the egiptians iewelles of syluer and gowlde, as god commawnded them soo to doo. Davyd, in the days of Abiather the hygh preste, did cume into *the* temple *and* dyd steale the hallowed breede; *and* yet god saide, "Dauid is a mañ euen after myne owne harte." Chryste hym selfe, whan he was here on the arthe, did take an asse *and* a cowlte *that* was none of hys; *and* yow knowe that god said of hym, "this is my beloued soone, in whome I delighte." thus yow may see that god delightithe in theves. but moste of all I marvell *that* men can dispyse yow theves, where as in all poyntes almoste yow be lyke vnto christe hym selfe: for chryste had noo dwellynge place; noo more haue yow. christe wente frome towne to towne; *and* soo doo yow. christe was hated of all men, sauynge of his freendes; and soo are yow. christe was laid waite vpon in many places; *and* soo are yow. chryste at the lengthe was cawght; *and* soo shall yow bee. he was browght before the iudges; *and* soo shall yow bee. he was accused; *and* soo shall yow bee. he was condempned; *and* soo shall yow bee. he was hanged; *and* so shall yow bee. he wente downe into hell; *and* soo shall yow dooe. mary! in this one thynge yow dyffer frome hym, for he rose agayne *and* assendid into heauen; *and* soo shall yow neuer dooe, withowte godes greate mercy, which gode grawnte yow! to whome with the father, *and* the soone, *and* the hooly ghoste, bee all honore and glorye, for euer *and* euer. Amen!

Thus his sermon beinge endyd, they gaue hym his money agayne that thay tooke frome hym, *and* ij⁵ to drynke for hys sermon.

finis.

[*The parts added to* HARMAN'S CAUEAT *to make*]
THE
Groundworke of Conny-catching;
the manner of their Pedlers-French, and the meanes
to vnderstand the same, with the cunning slights
of the Counterfeit Cranke.
Therein are handled the practises of the *Visiter*, the Fetches
of the Shifter and Rufflar, the deceits of their Doxes, the deuises
of Priggers, the names of the base loytering Losels, and
the meanes of euery Blacke-Art-mans shifts, with
the reproofe of all their diuellish
practises.
Done by a Justice of Peace of great authoritie, who hath
had the examining of diuers of them.

Printed at London by Iohn Danter for William Barley, and are to
be sold at his shop at the vpper end of Gratious streete,
ouer against Leaden-hall, 1592.

[leaf 2] ## To the gentle Readers health.

Gentle reader, as there hath beene diuers bookes set forth, as warnings for all men to shun the craftie coossening sleights of these both men and women that haue tearmed themselues Conny-catchers; so amongst the rest, bestow the reading ouer of this booke, wherin thou shalt find the ground-worke of Conny-catching, with the manner of their canting speech, how they call all things in their language, the horrible coossening of all these loose varlots, and the names of them in their seuerall degrees,

  First, The Visiter.   12. *A Dommerar.*
  2. *The Shifter.*   13. *A Dronken Tinkar.*
  3. *The Rufflar.*   14. *A Swadder, or Pedler.*
  4. *The Rogue.*   15. *A Iarkeman & Patrico.*
  5. *The wild Rogue.*   16. *A demander for glimmar.*
  6. *A prigger of Prauncers.*   17. *The baudy Basket.*
  7. *A Pallyard.*   18. *An Autem Mort.*
  8. *A Frater.*   19. *A walking Mort.*
  9. *An Abraham man.*   20. *A Doxe.*
 10. *A freshwater Marriner, or*   21. *A Dell.*
   Whipiacke.   22. *Kinchin Mort.*
 11. *A counterfait Cranke.*   23. *A Kinchin Co.*

All these playing their coossenings in their kinde are here set downe, which neuer yet were disclosed in anie booke of Conny-catching.

[leaf 2, back] A new kind of shifting sleight, practised at this day by *some of this Cony-catching crue, in Innes or vitualling houses, but especially in Faires or Markets,* which came to my hands since the imprinting of the rest.

Whereas of late diuers coossening deuises and deuilish deceites haue beene discouered, wherby great inconueniences haue beene eschewed, which otherwise might haue beene the vtter ouerthrowe of diuers honest men of all degrees, I thought this, amongst the rest, not the least worthie of noting, especially of those that trade to Faires and Markets, that therby being warned, they may likewise be armed, both to see the deceit, and shun the daunger. These shifters will come vnto an Inne or vittailing house, that is most vsed in the towne, and walke vp and downe; and if there come any gentleman or other, to lay vp either cloke, sword, or any other thing woorth the hauing, then one of this crue taketh the marks of the thing, or at least the token the partie giueth them: anone, after he is gone, he likewise goeth forth, and with a great countenance commeth in againe to the mayde or seruant, calling for what another left: if they doubt to deliuer it, then hee frets, and calles them at his pleasure, and tels them the markes and tokens: hauing thus done, hee blames their forgetfulnes, and giues them a couple of pence to buy them pinnes, bidding them fetch it straight, and know him better the next time, wherewith they are pleasd, and he possest of his pray. Thus one gotte a bagge of Cheese the last Sturbridge Faire; for in such places (as a reclaimd fellow of that crue confessed) they make an ordinary practise of the same.

[*The Pedler's French* follows, taken word for word from Harman's book, p. 82-7 above.]

[leaf 5] THE VISITER.

An honest youth, not many yeares since, seruant in this City, had leaue of his master at whitsontide to see his friends, who dwelt some fifty miles from London. It hapned at a Country wake, his mother and hee came acquainted with a precise scholler, that, vnder colour of strickt life, hath bin reputed for that hee is not: hee is well knowen in Paules Churchyard, and hath beene lately a visiting in Essex; for so he presumes to tearme his cosening walks : and therefore wee will call him here a Visiter. This honest seeming man must needes (sith his iourney lay to London) stay at the yong mans mothers all the holy daies : where as on his desert hee was kindly vsed; at length, the young man, hauing receiued his mother's blessing, with other his friendes giftes, amounting to some ten poundes, was to this hypocrite as to a faithful guide committed, and toward London they ride : by the way this Visiter discourses how excellent insight he had in Magick, to recouer by Art anything lost or stolne. Well, to sant Albons they reach; there they sup together, and, after the carowsing of some quarts of wine, they go to bed, where they kindly sleepe,—the Visiter slily, but the young man soundly. Short tale to make—out of his bed-fellow's sleeue this Visiter conuaid his twenty Angels, besides some other od siluer, hid it closely, and so fell to his rest. Morning comes—vp gets this couple—immediately the money was mist, much adoo was made; the Chamberlaine with sundry other seruants examined; and so hot the contention, that the good man, for the discharge of his house, was sending for a Constable to haue them both first searcht, his seruants Chests after. In the meane time the Visiter cals the yong man aside, and bids him neuer grieue, but take horse; and he warrants him, ere they be three miles out of towne, to helpe him to his money by Art, saying :—" In these Innes ye see how we shall be out-faced, and, beeing vnknowne, how euer we be wrongd, get little remedy." The yong man, in good hope, desired him to pay the reckoning, which done, together they ride. Being some two miles from the towne, they ride out of the ordinary way : there he tels this youth how vnwilling hee was to enter into the action, but that it was lost in his company, and so forth. Well, a Circle was made, wondrous words were vsed, many muttrings made : at length hee cries out,—" vnder a greene turfe, by the East side of an Oake; goe thither, goe thither." This thrice he cryed so ragingly, as the yuong man gest him mad, and was with feare almost beside himself. At length, pausing, quoth this Visiter, " heard ye nothing cry?" " Cry!" said the yong man, " yes; [leaf 5, back] you cride so as, for twise ten pound, I would not heare ye again." "Then," quoth he, "'tis all well, if ye remember the words." The yong man repeated them. With that this shifter said, "Go to the furthest Oke in the high-way towards S. Albons, and vnder a greene turfe, on the hither side, lyes your mony, and a note of his name that stole it. Hence I cannot stirre till you returne; neyther may either of our horses be vntide for that time : runne yee must not, but keepe an ordinary pace." Away goes the yong man gingerly ; and, being out of sight, this copesmate takes his cloke-bag, wherein was a faire sute of apparel, and, setting spurres to his horse, was, ere the Nouice returned, ridde cleane out of his view. The yong man, seeing himselfe so coossened, made patience his best remedie, tooke his horse, and came to London, where yet it was neuer his lucke to meet this visiter.

A SHIFTER.

A Shifter, not long since, going ordinarily booted, got leaue of a Carrier to ride on his owne hackney a little way from London, who, comming to the Inne where the Carier that night should lodge, honestly set vp the horse, and entred the hal, where were at one table some three and thirty clothiers, all returning to their seuerall countries. Vsing, as he could, his curtesie, and being Gentleman-like attirde, he was at all their instance placed at the vpper end by the hostesse. After hee had a while eaten, he fel to discourse with such pleasance, that all the table were greatly delighted therewith. In the midst of supper enters a noise of musitions, who with their instruments added a double delight. For them hee requested his hostesse to laye a shoulder of mutton and a couple of capons to the fire, for which he would pay, *and* then mooued in their behalfe to gather. Among them a noble was made, which he fingring, was well blest ; for before he had not a crosse, yet he promist to make it vp an angel. To be short, in comes the reckoning, which (by reason of the fine fare *and* excesse of wine) amounted to each mans halfe crown. Then hee requested his hostesse to prouide so many possets of sacke, as would furnish the table, which he would bestow on the Gentlemen to requite their extraordinary costs : *and* iestingly askt if she would make him her deputie to gather the reckoning; she graunted, and he did so: and on a sodaine, (faining to hasten his hostesse with the possets) he tooke his cloke, and, finding fit time, hee slipt out of doores, leauing the guestes and their hostesse to a new reckoning, *and* the musitians to a good supper, but they paid for the sauce. This iest some vntruly attribute to a man of excellent parts about London, but he is slandered: the party that performed it hath scarce any good qualitie to liue. Of these sort I could set downe a great number, but I leaue you now vnto those which by Maister Harman are discouered.

[Then follows Harman's book, commencing with a Ruffelar, p. 29. The woodcut of Nicolas Blunt and Nicolas Geninges (p. 50, above) is given, and another one representing the Cranke after he was stripped and washed. The volume ends with the chapter "Their vsage in the night," p. 76-8 above,—the woodcuts and verses at the end of Harman's book being omitted in the present *Groundworke of Conny-catching*. The last words in the latter are, " And this must the poore Farmer suffer, or els they threaten to burne him, and all that he hath."]

INDEX.

Abraham men, those who feign madness, 3; one of them, named Stradlynge, 'the craftiest and moste dyssemblyngest knaue,' 47
Altham, a curtall's wife, 4
Arsenick, to make sores with, 44
associate, accompany, 53
Autem, a church, 67, 83
—— Mortes, description of, 67; as chaste as Harman's 'Cowe,' 67
Awdeley, Iohn, a printer, 1
Awdeley's *Vacabondes;* Harman's references to, 20, 60
Axiltrye, casting of the, 46

baken, bacon, 3
baudy banquet, whoring, 63
bauer, ? band, 52
Bawd Phisicke, a cook, 14
Bawdy baskets, description of, 65; a story of one who, with an upright man, spoiled a poor beggar of his money, 66
beggar by inheritance, 42
belly chere, food, 32
belly chete, an apron, 83
benat, better, 86
bene, good, 83
bene bowse, good drink, 59
beneship, very well, 86

benshyp, very good, 83, 86
beray, dung, 13; dirty, 52
beteled, ? (*betelled* is deceived), 67
Bethlem Hospital, 52, 53
Blackheath, 77
bletinge chete, a calf or sheep, 83
Blunt, Nicolas, an upright man, 50, 87
bong, purse, 84, 86
booget, a bag, 59
bord, a shilling, 83
——, half a, sixpence, 83
borsholders, 21, *n.*, superior constables. See Halliwell's *Glossary*.
bottell, bundle, truss, 72
Bottomelye, Besse, a harlot, 75
bousing ken, an ale-house, 83
bowle, drink bowls of liquor, 32
bowse, drink, 32, 83; *v.* to drink, 84
braste, burst, 73
Bridewell, 57, 87
broused, bruised, 29
bryberinge, stealing, 60
Buckes, baskets, 21
Buckingham, Duke of, beheaded, 22
bufe, a dog, 84
bung, a purse, 83, 84, 86

buskill, ? bustle, wriggle, 15
bychery, 67
bycherye, whoring, 61
byd, pray, 15
byng a waste, go you hence, 84

cakling chete, a cock, or capon, 83
can skyl, know, 8
cante, to speak, 84
Canting, the language of vagabonds, 23; list of words, 82-4; specimen of, 84-6
Capcases, covers for caps, small bandboxes, 65
Capon hardy, 12. For 'capron hardy,' ' a notable whipster or twigger,' a bold or saucy young scamp. (See the Index to Caxton's *Book of Curtesye*, E. E. T. Soc., p. 54.)
cassan, cheese, 83
caster, a cloak, 82
casting of the sledge, 46
Caueat, a warning, 17
Chafe litter, the knave, described, 13
chafer, heating dish, 59
Charing Cross, 58
chattes, the gallows, 84, 86
Chayne, a gentleman, 58
Cheapside, 57, 87
Cheatours, card-sharpers enticing young men to their hosteries, win their money and depart, 7
cheeke by cheeke (now 'by jowl'), 12
chete, animal, 83, col. 2, foot
chetes, things, 42
Choplogyke, description of, 15
Christ, like a thief, 94, 95
Christes Hospital, 8
Clapperdogens, 44. *See* Palliardo.
Clement's Inn, 53

clocke, a cloak, 55
clyme three tres with a ladder, to ascend the gallows, 31
cly the gerke, to be whipped, 84
Cole, false, 15. (See Mr R. Morris in *Notes and Queries*, Oct., 1869, on *Colfox*, &c.
Cole Prophet, description of, 15
commission, a shirt, 83
Commitour of Tidings, a tell-tale, 14
common, commune, 45
conneys, rabbits, 35
conneyskins, rabbitskins, 65
connizance, cognizance, 35
Cornwall, 48
Cory fauell, a knave, described, 16
couch a hogshead, lie down and sleep, 77, 84
Counterfet Crankes, description of, 51; story of one that Harman watched, 51; how he was dressed, 51; his refusal to wash when bidden, 52; gives the name of Genings, 52; said he had been in Bethlehem Hospital, 52, which Harman found to be a lie, 53; in the middle of the day he goes into the fields and renews the blood on his face, 53; what money he received, 53; at night he goes to Newington, where he is given in charge, 54; the amount of his gains, 55; his escape, 55; his recapture, 56, *n.*; his punishment, 57, *n.*
Cousoners, cheaters, 1
Crashing chetes, teeth, 82
crassinge chetes, apples, pears, or any other fruit, 84
Cross Keys Inn in Cranford (Middlesex) or Crayford (Kent), 77
cuffen, fellow, 86. *See* Quyer.
Cursetors, 17; explanation of, 27

Curtal, 37
Curtall, one who is next in authority to an upright man, 4
Curtesy man, described, 6
cutte, to say, 84
cutte bene whydds, speak or give good words, 84
cutte benle, speak gently, 84
cutte quyre whyddes, give evil words or evil language, 84

darkemans, night, 84
Dartford, 58
David, a thief, 94, 95
ded lyft, a; last refuge, 34
Dells, rogues' virgins, described, 75
Demaunder for glymmar, description of, 61; story of one who behaved courteously to one man and uncourteously to another, 61—65
Deptford, 77
Desmond, Earl of, 82
Devil's Pater noster, 15
Devonshire, 48
dewse a vyle, the country, 84, 86
Dialogue, between upright man and rogue, 84—87
dokte, fornicated with, 87
Dommerar, description of, 57; of one who was made to speak, and afterwards punished on the pillory, 58, 59
doson, dozen, 34
Doxes, description of, 4, 6, 73
Draw-the-pudding-out-of-the-fire; a beggars' inn at Harrow-on-the-Hill, 77
drawers, hosen, 83
Drawlatches, a class of beggars, 27
Dronken Tinckar, description of, 59
drouselye, drowsily, 76

dudes, cloths, 83
dup the gyger, open the door, 84
Dyng-thrift, description of, 15

Egiptians, description of, 23
Esau, a thief, 94, 95
Esaye, Isaiah, 24
Esen Droppers, eaves-droppers, 15
exonerate, empty (one's belly), 55

factors, tax-gatherers, 45
fambles, hands, 82; famble, 87
fambling chete, ring on the hand, 82
Faytores, a class of beggars, 27
ferres, 35, ferries
Filtchman, the truncheon of a staff, 4
Fingerers, 7—9. *See* Cheatours.
for knowing; against, to prevent, being recognized, 71
flagg, a groat, 83, 85
flebytinge, 73
fictinge Fellowshyp, the company of vagabonds, 24
Frater, one who goes with a licence to beg for some Spittlchouse or Hospital, but who usually robs poor women, 4; description of, 45
Freshwater Mariner, description of, 48
Furmenty, 22
fustian fume, 46
fylche, to beat, to rob, 84
fylthy firy flankard, 29
fynesed, finished, 70
Fyngerer, 8, 9

gage, a quart pot, 83
—— of bowse, a quart of drink, 34
gally slopes, breeches, 35
gan, a mouth, 82

gealy gealowsit, good fellowship, 55
gentry cofes ken, a noble or gentleman's house, 83
gentry morte, a noble or gentlewoman, 84
Genynges, Nicolas, a counterfeit cranke, 50, 87
gestes, guests, 61
Glasyers, eyes, 82
glimmeringe morte, a woman who travels the country begging, saying her goods have been burnt, 61
glymmar, fire, 61, 83
grannam, corn, 83
Grauesend barge, a resort of vagabonds and knaves, 1
graunt, agree, 53
greffe, grief, 55
Grene Winchard, description of a, 14
Groundworke of Conny-catching, 97
grunting chete, or patricos kynchen, a pig, 83
Gryffith, Wylliam, a printer, 17
Gybe, a licence, 4; a writing, 83
gygger, a door, 83, 85
Gyle Hather, description of, 14
gyllot, a whore, 71

Haben, a witty parson, 92
hande charcher, handkerchief, 72
Harman beck, constable, 84
Harman, Thomas, his *Caveat*, 17-91; epistle to the reader, 27; his old tenant, 30; his copper cauldron stolen, 35; recovered, 35; notice to tinkers of the loss of his cauldron, 35; his gelding stolen, 44; in commission of the peace, 60; paid for beggars' secrets, 74
Harmans, the stocks, 84
Harrow-on-the-Hill, inn at, 77

Hartley Row in Hampshire, 92, 93
Hearing chetes, ears, 82
heauing of the bowth, robbing the booth, 4
Helpers of rogues, 9
Helycon, 28
heue a bough, rob a booth, 84
Hill's, Mr, Rents, 57
him redundant: leapes him, 43, l. 24
Hoker, or Angglear, description of, 35; anecdote of one who took the clothes of the bed in which 3 men were sleeping, without awaking them, 36
Holborn, 54
hollowe hosteler, 63
horse locke, 39
hosen, breeches, 71, 72
hosted, lodged, 57, *n.*
hosteries, card-sharpers' resorts, 9
House of Pity, inn in Northall, 77
hoyssed, hoisted, 20
huggeringe, loitering, 43
Hyberdyne, a parson, 93
hygh, hie, 33
hygh pad, highway, 84

Jacob, a thief, 94, 95
Iarckeman, a maker of counterfeit licences, 5, 60
Iarckes, seals, 4
Iarke, a seal, 83
ich, I, 8
Jeffrey Gods Fo, a liar, 13
Ingratus, an ungrateful knave, 16
in printe, meaning 'correct,' 45
Iockam, yard, penis, 87
iompe, jump, plump, exactly, 44

Irishe toyle, a beggar, 5
Irish rogues, 44, 48
Isleworth (Thystellworth), St Julian's, a beggars' inn at, 77
Iusticers, Justices, 21

Karle, a knave, 8
ken, a house, 83, 84, 86
Kent, a man of worship in, death of, 22
Kent, mentioned, 37, 43, 48, 61, 63, 66, 68, 77
Kent St, Southwark, 57
Ketbroke, a beggars' inn, near Blackheath, 77
kinde, nature, 52
Kitchen Co, a boy, 5, 76
——— Morte, a girl, 5, 76
Knapsbery (inn near London), 77
Knaues, 25 orders of, 1
———, quartern of, 1
Kynges barne, beggars' inn in Kent, 77

lage, water, 83
lag of dudes, a bucke of clothes, 83
lap, butter, milk, or whey, 83
lasy Lorrels, 82
lecherous husband cured, 68-73
Leicester, 56
lewed lecherous loyteringe, 31
lewtering Luskes, 82
licoryce knaue, a drunkard, 13
lightmans, day, 84
(Lincoln's Inn) Fields, 53
London, 30, 42, 49
lousey leuterars, vagabonds, 22
lowhinge chete, a cow, 83
lowre, money, 83, 85, 86
Lubbares, lubbers, 47

luckly, lucky, 19
Ludgate, 57
lybbege, a bed, 83
lybbet, a stick, 26
lykinge, lustful, 21
Lynx eyes, 54. (See Index to Hampole's *Pricke of Conscience*.)
Lypken, a house to lie in, 83

make, halfpenny, 83
make (think) it strange, 41
makes, mates, 23
mammerings, mumblings, 72
manerly marian, 62
margery prater, a hen, 83
Mariner, one at Portsmouth the maker of counterfeit licences for Freshwater mariners, 49
matche of wrastlinge, 46
maunde, ask or require, 84, 85
Messenger, Ione, an honest bawdy basket, 65
Milling of the ken, sending children into houses to rob, 67
mofling chete, a napkin, 83
mounched, eat, 72
mounch-present, one who, being sent by his master with a present, must taste of it himself, 14
myll a ken, rob a house, 84
mynt, gold, 83

Nab, a head, 82, 86
Nabchet, a hat or cap, 82
nase, drunken, 86
Newhaven, 67
Newington, 54, 56
Nichol Hartles, a coward, 13
Northall, beggars' inn at, 77
nosegent, a nun, 83
nouels, news, 14
Nunquam, a loitering servant, 16

nygle, haue to do with a woman carnally, 84
nyp a boung, to cut a purse, 84

Obloquium, a malapert knave, 13
occupying, holding of land, 38
of, off, 39
oysters of East Kent, 68

Palliards, description of, 4, 44; doings of, 44; list of names of, 81, 82
pannam, bread, 83
Param, milk, 83, n.
patrico, a priest, 6, 60
paulmistrie, fortune-telling, 23
pecke, meat, 86
peddelars Frenche. See Canting.
pek, meat, 83
peld pate, head uncovered, 34
pelte, clothes, 76
peltinge, ? paltry, contemptible, 20
Penner, a pen-case, 54
pens, pence, 55
pickthanke knaue, 14
pillory in Cheapside, 57
pitching of the barre, 46
pity: it pytied him at the hart, 41
poppelars, porridge, 83
porte sale, ? quick sale, 77
Portsmouth, 49
Poules, St Paul's, 8
prat, a buttocke, 82
prating knaue, 15
pratling chete, a tongue, 82
prauncer, a horse, 83
Prigger of Paulfreys, a stealer of horses, 4
Proctour, a liar, 14; keeper of a spittlehouse, 45

PROVERBS:
  although Truth be blamed, it shall never be shamed, 28
  as the begger knowes his dishe, 32
  don't wake the sleeping dog, 73
  God hath done his part, 48
  out of sight, out of minde, 32
  swete meate wyll haue sowre sawce, 72
prygge, to ride, 84
Prygger of Prauncers, description of, 42; a story of a gentleman who lost his horse by giving it in charge for a short time to a 'priggar,' 43
Prygges, tinkers, 59
Prygman, one who steals clothes off hedges, and a robber of poultry, 3

quakinge chete, or red shanke, a drake or duck, 83
quaromes, a body, 82
Queen Elizabeth, 21
quier, nought, 83
Quier crampringes, bolts or fetters, 84, 86
Quire bird, one lately come out of prison, 4
quyer cuffyn, justice of the peace, 84, 86
Quyerkyn, prison house, 84, 86

rabblement, 19
rakehelles, 19
Ratsbane, 44
rechles, reckless, 15
rifflinge, 32
Rince pytcher, a drunkard, 13
Ring chopper, description of, 11
—— faller, description of, 10
Robardesmen, robbers, 27. See William of Nassington's description of them quoted in *Notes & Queries* by F. J. F., 1869; and *The Vision of Piers Plowman*, ed. Wright, ii. 506, 521.

INDEX.

Robin goodfelow, 36
Rochester, 66
Rogeman, a receiver of stolen clothes, 3
Roger, or tyb of the buttery, a goose, 83
Roges, description of, 36; subject to beastly diseases, 37; list of names of, 80, 81
Rogues, a story of two, who made the acquaintance of a parson at an ale-house, and afterwards went to his house and robbed him, 37
Rome bouse, wine, 83
Rome mort, the Queen, 84
Rome vyle, London, 84
Rothered in Kent, 77
rowsey, ? rough, or frowzy, 19
Royal Exchange, 8
roylynge, travelling, 31
ruffe, rough, 33
Ruffeler, a robber of 'wayfaring men and market women,' 3, 29; a story of one who robbed an old man, a tenant of Harman's, on Blackheath, 30
ruffian cly the, devil take thee, 84
ruffian, to the, 84, to the devil
ruffmans, woods or bushes, 84
ruff pek, bacon, 83
ruysting, roystering, 32

Salomon, an altar, or mass, 83
sawght, sought, 62
Saynt Augustyn, 24
scelorous, wicked, 20
sewerly, surely, 50
Shifters, 1
shotars hyl, Shooter's Hill, 30
Shreeues, sheriffs, 21
Shrewd turne, ? sharp handling, hard usage, 15

Shrewsbury, Elizabeth Countess of, Harman's dedication to, 19
shrodge, shrugged, hugged, 71
Simon soone agon, a loitering knave, 13
skew, a cup, 83
Skoller, a waterman (and his boat), 54
skower the cramprings, wear bolts or fetters, 84
skypper, a barn, 83
slates, sheets to lie in, 61, 76, 77, 83
small breefe, old briefe of vacabonds, meaning Awdeley's book, 20
smell feastes, 46
smelling chete, a nose, 82; a garden or orchard, 84
snowte fayre, fair-faced, 61
sod, boiled, 22
Somersetshire, 61
soup, chewed, to produce foaming at the mouth, 51
Spanlles, spaniel-dogs, 33
Spearwort, 44
Spice-cakes, 12
spitlehouse, 45; row in a, 45; the constable wants to take in custody the roysterers, 46; the good wife of the house intreats him for her guests, and while so doing the next door neighbours enter the kitchen, and steal the supper that she was preparing, 46
squaymysh, squeamish, 55
St. George's Fields, 54
St. Giles's in the Fields, 54
St. Julian's (inn in Thystellworth; Isleworth), 77
St. Quinten's (inn near London), 77
St. Tybbe's (inn near London), 77
stall, to make or ordain, 84

INDEX.   111

stalling to the rogue, ceremony of, 34
stampers, shoes, 83
stampes, legs, 82
Statutes, i. Edw. VI. c. iii, p. 20, *n.*; xxvii. Hen. VIII. for punishment of vagabonds, 29
staulinge ken, a house that will receive stolen wares, 32, 83
stibber gibber knaue, a liar, 14
stow you, hold your peace, 84
Stradlynge, an Abraham man, 47
strommell, straw, 83
Sturton, Lord, 48
summer-games, 47
surgeon, who strung up the dumb rogue, 58-9
Swadders and Pedlers, description of, 60
Swygman, a pedlar, 5

tempering, tampering, 70
Temple Bar, 53
'Thank God of all,' 67 (cp. Shakspere's 'Thank God you are rid of a knave.' *Much Ado,* iii. 3.)
the, thee, 55
Thieves, a sermon in praise of, 92
'Three trees,' the gallows, 31
tickle in the ear, gammon, 9
Tinkard, a beggar, 5
tiplinge[house], an ale-house, 40
tittiuell knaue, a tale-bearer, 15
togeman, a coat, 77, 82
tortylles, turtle-doves, lovers, 62
towre, see, 84, 85
trashe, goods, 77
trininge, hanging, the end of roges, 37, 84
Troll and troll by, a knave, described, 12

Troll Hazard of Trace, a knave, 12
Troll Hazard of tritrace, a knave, 13
Troll with, a knave, 12
Truth, proverb as to, 28
tryninge, hanging, 84
twin'd hempe, rope and gallows, 29 (cp. Bulleyn in *The Babees Book,* p. 240-3)
Two Gent. of Verona, 45
Tynckars, Harman sends notice of the stealing of his cauldron to the, 35
typ, secret, 20
typlinge houses, alehouses, 24

Vacabonde—one being caught, and brought before the justices of the peace, promised to tell them the names and degrees of his fellows, on condition that he escaped punishment, which being granted, he fulfilled his promise, and Awdeley obtained the materials for his book, 2
Vacabondes, beggerly, 1; ruflyng, 1; 'the old briefe' of, 60
Vagabondes, their vsage in the night, 76
Vagabonds, account of the doings of, at the funeral of a man of worship in Kent, 22
vagarantes, 19
Vngracious, a man who will not work, 15
Vnthrift, a reckless knave, 15
vntrus, to undress, 72
Vpright man, description of, 1, 4, 31
Vpright men, list of the names of, 78, 79, 80
Vrmond, Earle of, 82

walkinge mortes, description of, 67; a story of a trick that one played on a man who would have

INDEX.

had to do with her, and the punishment he received instead, 67—73
wannion, a curse, 62
wappinge, fornicating, 87
Washman, one who shams lameness, sickness, etc., 5
waste, bynge a; go hence, 84, 86
watch, the constable, 45
watche, person, 61; our watche, us, 86
Welsh rogues, 44, 57
Whistle, anecdote of the, 61-5
Whipiacke, a robber of booths and stalls, 4
Whitefriars, 51, 56
whydds, words, 84, 86
whystell, whistle, 62
whyte money, silver, 42

wilde roge, description of, 41; story of one robbing a man, of whom he had just begged, 42
wilde roge's reason for being a beggar, 42
windless, out of breath, 73
windshaken knaue, 66
woode, mad, 14
Wostestowe, a servant of the Lord Keeper's, 58
wyld Dell, description of, 75
wyn, a penny, 83

yannam, bread, 83, *n.*
yaram, milk, 83
yemen, yeomen, 22
ynkell, tape, 65

The manufacturer's authorised representative in the EU for product safety is Oxford University Press España S.A. of El Parque Empresarial San Fernando de Henares, Avenida de Castilla, 2 - 28830 Madrid (www.oup.es/en or product.safety@oup.com). OUP España S.A. also acts as importer into Spain of products made by the manufacturer.
Printed and bound by CPI Group (UK) Ltd, Croydon, CR0 4YY

20/03/2026

02075337-0016